MW01178668

HOW TO MAKE BIG

WITHOUT LEAVING YOUR KITCHEN

A Homemakers Guide

To

Moneymaking Opportunities

By Karen Kraft and Anthony Besser

©1996 Karen Kraft & Anthony Besser
All rights reserved.
Published in the United States by The Magni Group, Inc.
P.O. Box 849, McKinney, TX 75070
Printed in the United States of America

All rights reserved. No part of this publication may be reproduced,
stored in a retrieval system, or transmitted, in any form or by any
means, electronic, mechanical, photocopying, recording or otherwise without the prior permission of the publisher.

Illustration by Corel Gallery 2

ISBN 1-882330-47-1

Congratulations! You have just taken the first step toward starting your own business.

Don't let anyone tell you that NOW is not a good time to start a business. NOW is ALWAYS the BEST time to start your own business.

In this book, we have given you many ideas for starting a business. Remember, all it takes is ONE GOOD IDEA! The best business for you would be one that you truly love, however, if you find one that you just like a lot and can see the profit potential in it, it may be the one for you.

You will notice that there is no table of contents. This is a deliberate decision. Why? As we stated, you only need **one** good idea for your new business, so we don't want you to pre-judge any of the opportunities in this book. Instead, consider them all...then decide.

We have also placed the chapters on "Things You'll Have To Do To Start Your Business" and "Advertising And Marketing Your Business" at the end of the book. Why? Because at this exact moment, the important issue is to FIND a business that you want to start!

The most important thing that you should keep in mind is that after you have selected a business and spent a reasonable time researching it, then you must take the most important step in any business...**JUST DO IT !!**

Table of Contents

GUIDE

TO

STARTING

YOUR

WHOLESALE

BUSINESS

A GUIDE TO STARTING
YOUR WHOLESALE BUSINESS

Congratulations! You have decided on a business opportunity that not only interests you, but has a good profit potential. Now you are saying to yourself, "what do I do next?"

If you have decided to sell wholesale (selling to other wholesalers, distributors or merchants in bulk at a below retail price), or you wish to combine wholesale with retail, the following steps will serve as a good guide.

You have selected a business. Ask yourself these questions?

Does this business opportunity really appeal to you enough to hold your interest in the good times as well as the bad?

Have you sat down and put pen to paper, to see what is the least amount of money (and potentially the most amount of money) that you could make from this business?

Do you have the skills, talent and knowledge to do this business or are you willing to acquire it?

Determine how much money you will need to start the business.

> How much money will you need for:

>> equipment (other than what you currently have)
>> inventory (your starting stock)
>> advertising
>> supplies (office, etc.)
>> vehicles (may be specialized)

ARE YOU STILL WITH US?????   GOOD!!!

As a wholesaler is there a demand for your product?

> **Price**

> Will the price of your product make it attractive and offer your wholesale customers sufficient room for them to in turn, sell it at a good profit?

> Can you keep your product cost consistent in order to allow you to wholesale at a consistent price?

> Can you undersell your competition?

> **Quality**

> Can you provide better quality products for the same price, or better than your competition?

> Can you provide a better quality product... period?

Can you provide a lower quality product, but still good, for a less expensive market?

Is the quality of your product consistent?

Can you (or your supplier) handle an increase in your business without sacrificing quality?

Service

Can you deliver what you have promised?

If a problem occurs, can you explain the situation to your customers?

In order to satisfy your customers, if a temporary problem arises, are you willing to find new suppliers, even if it reduces or negates your profit, until the situation is corrected.

Now that we've considered most of the important factors of wholesaling, we need to find out if we have a potentially viable business before we invest our hard earned money in it. The easiest way to do this is to contact potential customers directly.

Look in the yellow pages for potential customers. (You are looking for business that will retail your products to the public {and if your prices are low enough}, other wholesalers and distributors.

Phone them and speak to the owners or buyers.

Tell them what you are selling and why they should buy from you (ie. price, quality or service...or any combination of the above.)

If they are interested, make an appointment to see them or arrange to mail them samples.

If they like your product and wish to place an order, see if you can get a contract to sell them X number of pieces over a given time span.

The benefit to you...you have a customer/sales locked in.

Tell them that their advantage is a fixed price for a given length of time.

After you have contacted a significant number of potential customers, you should be able to determine if there is a market for you.

Note: it is important to understand that as a wholesaler, your customers are in business to make money and are therefore relying on you and your product/s. Your key should be... providing reliable, consistent and honest service to them! If you let them down, you are putting their business at risk and they are therefore unlikely to continue doing business with you.

Now that you have determined that there is really a market, lets' get the boring paperwork out of the way.

a) Register your business name (DBA) usually at your county clerks office.
b) Obtain a re-sale permit/sales tax number, if necessary.
c) Open a business bank account.

d) Get business cards printed up (and stationary, if necessary)
e) Set up a bookkeeping system, or get an accountant. You can do this now or later. Consider speaking with an attorney, if you have legal questions.

Take number 3 and expand it, finding more customers for your product.

Purchase any inventory, equipment, and supplies necessary to begin your business (keep your overhead...expenditures...as low as possible. Becoming established in business can take time. The longer that you are around, the greater your chance for success. Remember that you are in business to make money, not spend it! Just look at the big companies who have recently downsized, and economized, in order to stay in business.)

Give good service...if you do, the customers that you begin with will not only stay with you but can bring you more customers.

How do you make your business grow?

Advertise

Advertise in trade journals that are aimed at your business or product.

Contact more and more business, not only within your own city, but in other areas as well.

Consider participating in trade shows, not only within your own industry, but in ancillary business as well.

Are you trying new offers or discounts?

Do you always have your business cards with you?

Expanding

Have you considered doing trade shows, conventions, etc.?

Have you checked into mail order?

Have you considered hiring outside sales people/reps and paying them a commission only?

Offer price breaks for larger orders and consistent orders (ie. monthly orders for 6 months, etc.)

Consider buying direct from the manufacturer or manufacturing the product/s yourself in order to reduce your costs. You can therefore increase your profit or chose to pass on some or all of the savings to your customers.

Consider locating and wholesaling to distributors in other cities in order to increase your wholesale market without increasing your costs.

Final Note: these guidelines should give you a logical progression on the route to starting and building your business. Never forget...**the most important key for getting any business started is to take your own desire to succeed and put it into action. In other words... DO IT!!**

GUIDE

TO

STARTING

YOUR

RETAIL

BUSINESS

A GUIDE TO STARTING
YOUR RETAIL BUSINESS

Congratulations! You have decided on a business opportunity that not only interests you, but has a good profit potential. Now you are saying to yourself, "what do I do next?"

Well, if you have decided that you want to sell directly to the public ("retail"), the following steps will serve as a guide to starting your successful business.

You have selected a business. Ask yourself these questions?

Does this business opportunity really appeal to you enough to hold your interest in the good times as well as the bad?

Have you sat down and put pen to paper, to see what is the least amount of money (and potentially the most amount of money) that you could make from this business?

Do you have the skills, talent and knowledge to do this business or are you willing to acquire it?

Determine how much money you will need to start the business.

How much money will you need for:

      equipment (other than what you currently
      have)
      inventory (your starting stock)
      advertising
      supplies (office, etc.)
      vehicles (may be specialized)

ARE YOU STILL WITH US????? GOOD!!!

We know that you're interested in your business...is anyone else going to be? (ie. Is there a market?) The purpose of this step is to make sure that people will buy your goods or services **before** you have invested a lot of time and money in your new venture. How do we do this?

Advertise...

What methods of advertising are successful in your area?
(ie. newspapers, flyers, bulletin board notices, etc.)

What are the most inexpensive, and yet effective?
(Consider where you live, city or rural, and what type of advertising will reach your potential customers most effectively.)

      The purpose of your advertising at this stage is to get a response, either a phone or mail response. In order to get a response:

Describe your product or service (in detail if it's not obvious).

Definitely include the price of your product or service.

Inform your customers that it's a new business (don't state that you are just testing for interest).

Have an introductory special offer (ie. reduced price, special coupon, buy one get one free, a free gift, etc.).

Don't forget to include your address or phone number.

Keep in mind that one ad on its own usually will not give you a true picture of your market...only continued advertising will do that.

Now that you have determined that there is really a market, lets' get the boring paperwork out of the way.

a) Register your business name (DBA) usually at your county clerks office.
b) Obtain a re-sale permit/sales tax number, if necessary.
c) Open a business bank account.
d) Get business cards printed up (and stationary, if necessary)
e) Set up a bookkeeping system, or get an accountant. You can do this now or later. Consider speaking with an attorney, if you have legal questions.

Start your advertising for real.

Purchase any inventory, equipment, and supplies necessary to begin your business (keep your overhead...expenditures...as low as possible. Becoming established in business can take time. The longer that you are around, the greater your chance for success. Remember that you are in business to make money, not spend it! Just look at the big companies who have recently downsized, and economized, in order to stay in business.)

Give good service...if you do, the customers that you begin with will not only stay with you but can bring you more customers (referrals).

How do you make your business grow?

Advertise

Are you trying new ads? (new headlines, wording, etc.)

Have you tried new media...newspapers, bill boards, etc.?

Are you trying new offers or discounts?

Do you always have your business cards with you and do you regularly hand them out?

Referrals

Are you asking your present customers for referrals?

Are you offering incentives to your present customers for good referrals?

Are you asking your friends and family for referrals?

Are you asking the companies that you buy from for referrals?

Expanding

Do you wish to open a store?

Have you considered doing flea markets, trade shows, conventions, etc.?

Have you considered the possibility of leasing a push cart at a local mall?

Have you checked into mail order?

Have you considered hiring outside sales people/reps and paying them a commission only?

Final Note: these guidelines should give you a logical progression on the route to starting and building your business. Never forget...**the most important key for getting any business started is to take your own desire to succeed and put it into action. In other words... DO IT!!**

THINGS YOU'LL

HAVE TO DO

BEFORE STARTING

YOUR BUSINESS

THINGS YOU'LL HAVE TO DO
BEFORE STARTING YOUR BUSINESS

We have started numerous businesses between us and no matter what business you are setting up, there are several steps that you will have to complete. DO NOT LET THESE STEPS PUT YOU OFF! The following, may be considered boring or tedious, but they are necessary and if you plan well, most can be done in a single day.

Selecting A Name For Your Company: in order to start a company you will have to give it a name, either your own name or an assumed name. If you use your own name you won't have to register it, although we do recommend it. For an assumed name, you will have to go to the DBA office ("doing business as"). This is usually located at your country clerks office, but call before your go to make sure.

A note on selecting your name: pick a good name, one that describes what you are doing, or select a unique name.

When you go to the DBA office, you will have to search through their files, which are usually on computer or microfiche (some offices will do this for you.) You will have to go through the alphabetically listed names of companies to make sure that no one else is already using the name that you have selected. Once you have checked the business name you have selected is available, then you can go ahead and officially register it.

What type of company will you be setting up? There are three types of companies from which to choose...sole proprietorships, partnerships and corporations.

Sole Proprietorships: this is a business where you will be the only owner. This is usually the case in most businesses. Simply check "sole proprietorship" on the application and pay the small fee (usually between $5 and $10) that is required.

Partnerships: if you are forming your business with one or more people, it is usually best to do this in the form of a partnership. (If you do start a partnership, have all the details spelled out in a partnership agreement.   The   agreement   will   include   all responsibilities, how the money or profits is to be handled, the method that will be used to break up the company, should that be necessary, etc.) This can be drawn up by you, or by a lawyer. (Once you have selected "partnership" on the application and paid your fee, that is all that is required.)

Corporations: we don't recommend that you form a corporation at this stage.   Forming a corporation requires additional expenses and the advantages that you will gain from forming a corporation are usually more important after your company has grown. The best approach will be to incorporate after your business has grown to the stage where spending the additional money to incorporate will benefit you. When you reach this level, your lawyer, accountant, or company that specializes in forming corporations can give you advice on the best type of corporation to form for your specific needs.

SALES TAX

Whether or not you are going into retail, and therefore collect sales tax, you will need to get a sales tax permit. You will also need it to open a business bank account.

In order to get a sales tax permit, you will need to go to your local sales tax office (you can find this in the phone book). After you have registered your business name at the DBA office, you should go to the sales tax office, and apply for your permit. Take your DBA certificate with you. (You may be required to pay a fee at this time...this differs from state to state.) If you will be retailing, they will ask you to estimate your sales for the first quarter of business. **TIP:** if you do not have much money or do not want to put much money into your business at this time. Tell the sales tax office that you plan to do mostly wholesale. Why? Because wholesalers don't collect sales tax. Otherwise you may have to put up a bond with the sales tax office. When you do start retailing, you will have to collect sales tax and pay it on the schedule required by your sales tax office. We are in no way, suggesting that you do not collect sales tax on your retail sales but are rather suggesting a way that you can limit the amount of money that you have to come up with at the very beginning. The fact is, you don't know how much money your business will generate in the beginning. We all get excited about the possibilities of our new business and the money that we will earn. Frequently, when applying for a sales tax permit, people state that they expect to earn "x" dollars immediately, when in reality, they will only reach that level after they have been in the business for a few months or more. That is the question that they are asking you on the application. After you have been retailing for awhile, and **paying** your sales tax quarterly (or as determined by the sales tax office), they may require you to put up a bond but by then, you will have the money to pay it. We repeat...**Do collect and pay to the state, your sales tax on retail sales.** If they later ask you to put up a bond, you can explain that you have been collecting and paying them sales tax and that putting up a bond is not necessary.

OPENING A BUSINESS BANK ACCOUNT

After you have a DBA and sales tax permit, your next step should be to open a business bank account. In the same way that you shop for a personal bank account. Shop for a business bank account. Contact many banks, preferably by phone, and find out if they offer business accounts. Ask if there is a monthly service fee, ask if they charge for deposits or charge for writing checks on your account. Your whole goal is to find a bank that will handle your account for no fee, or as small a fee as possible. Remember that you are in business to make money for yourself, not to make money for the bank. Our tip: shop around, shop around, shop around!

WORKING OUT OF YOUR HOME

There are two major considerations when you are setting up a business out of your home. First...zoning. The area that you are living in may not allow you to run a business from your home. If it is a "low-key" business (ie. you don't have clients coming in and out of your home all day), and you don't advertise your business to your neighbors, odds are that no one else will notice. However, we recommend that you check with your local zoning office to see what their regulations are. In our area, we can operate a home business provided no clients come and go from our home and no business signs are posted. We can, however, put a business sign in the window. Secondly, the area that you live in (your subdivision) may have deed restrictions preventing your from having a home based business. If there is, you can operate a low-key business or tell some of your neighbors what you do, tell them there will not be lots of people coming to and from your home and ask for their approval. It is best to run a low-key, quiet business and not to disturb your neighbors or present any problems for them.

KEEPING YOUR BOOKS

Before you set up your business, you should have a good system to keep record of your sales and expenses. (ie. cost of purchases, cost of supplies, sales, sales tax, etc.) You can either purchase a good system at your local office supply store or there are many good systems available on software if you have a computer. (If you don't have a computer presently, consider purchasing one when you are financially able, get a good, **easy,** software package and life will be so much easier. Ask lots of questions before you buy anything. Don't let yourself be talked into buying a program that you'll never be able to use. Don't rely on the "hype" written in the advertisements by the software company. Go to, or call, a large company such as COMP USA, The Computer Warehouse, The Computer Store, etc., explain that you have no experience with a computer (or whatever level you are really at) and ask them to recommend a **simple** program, explain specifically what it will, and won't, do and recommend a more extensive program for later, as your skill level improves. The ideal program would be one that can be upgraded at a later date, into another program that offers more features. There are several on the market to from which to choose.

INSURANCE

Insurance may, or may not, be a consideration for you in the beginning. When you start your business, insurance will be primarily related to liability and to insure your stock/equipment. The first consideration should be whether you want to insure your equipment and stock. If you are working from home and will be there most of the time, your homeowners insurance may already cover everything. As you grow and your equipment becomes more expensive and your stock increases, this may become an issue. However, if you can afford to insure it now (or wish to do so), please do. Liability insurance, particularly if you are small and do not have any employees, and have no customers coming to your home, may be put off until your business grows. However, in both cases, you should consult with a good insurance agent to find out what the costs are and the advantages and disadvantages of purchasing insurance now and later on. Your insurance requirements may be very different if you have a business where you leave home for most of the time, take equipment away from your home, or have customers coming to your home on a regular basis.

EMPLOYEES

If you will be working this business on your own, or with members of your family, then none of the state and federal laws will apply to you. However, if you will be hiring employees now or in the future, you will need to check with both your Chamber of Commerce and your state employment commission, as to state and federal laws. These will include: the number of hours that employees are allowed to work, minimum wages, social security payments, employee taxes, employee insurance, working conditions, etc. Do not worry about these. If you can afford employees, it means that your business is growing and your accountant should be able to help you with most of these matters.

MONEY

Many of the businesses that we list require little or no money to get started. However, if you find yourself without funds to start this venture, some of the easiest ways to raise this money are as follows. You can always approach family or friends for short term loans, or sell them part of the business.

You can go to your bank and ask them for a line of credit. (A line of credit is a pre-approved loan from your bank that requires only your signature to withdraw funds. You can take out part or all of the line of credit and pay it back in small amounts.) Banks frequently have a $2,500 minimum line of credit. After you obtain a line of credit and have used it for 2 or 6 months, ask if it can be increased to $5,000 and increase it at regular intervals. If your bank doesn't give you a line of credit, go to several other banks and see if they will give you one.

This is one of the easiest ways to borrow, so we recommend that you find a bank that will give you a line of credit.

CREDIT CARDS

If you have **no other** avenue for immediate cash, you can always take a cash advance from your credit cards. You should be confident that you can pay this back within a short period of time since most credit cards charge an amazingly high interest rate (18%, 19%, 20%). But if you feel certain that you can pay back this cash advance, then you can do what many other people do...take a cash advance on your credit cards and start your business.

BANK LOANS

Bank loans, unlike lines of credit, require that you make specific application for a specific kind of loan, in this case, a loan for a small business. Do not be surprised if they turn you down. However, if you have excellent credit, a good history at your bank, a good work history, especially in the field of your new business, there is a good chance that the bank will give you a small loan. Try and get as low an interest rate as possible.

GETTING A LINE OF CREDIT FROM YOUR SUPPLIERS

If the money you will need to start your business is to purchase products from a manufacturer or wholesaler. Try phoning those manufacturers and wholesalers, explain what business you are in and that you are interested in buying from them. Then ask them what is required to get a credit line with them. Many of them will tell you that they do not give credit on first orders but you will be surprised by the number of wholesalers and manufacturers who will give you a 30 day line of credit if you give them 2 or 3 business references. Before calling these wholesalers/
manufacturers, talk to friends who own businesses and any local businesses that you have dealt with in the past. Tell them that you are starting a new business and ask them if you can use them as a reference. When you have found 3 people who are willing to do this, then you are ready to call your suppliers, giving these people as references.

Once you have a credit line from a manufacturer or wholesaler, work extra hard to pay off your invoice within the 30 days, so you must hustle, hustle, hustle and sell however much is necessary to pay off your credit line. By doing this, you will be able to expand your credit line and your business on a steady basis. Then use the first credit line as a reference to get other credit lines from other companies.

SBA LOANS

When you get a little bigger and are ready to expand, you can go to the SBA (Small Business Association) and ask them what their requirements are for obtaining a government backed SBA loan.   (The SBA is also a good source of free information for many aspects of starting a business and have many ideas on advertising, marketing, keeping records, etc. Feel free to call them. You can even go to their offices and talk to the retired business people who staff their offices and get valuable experience and information for free.

Now that we have covered most of the topics that you will need to take into consideration and follow through in order to set up your business, let me point out some of the benefits of your business.

Besides the short commute from your bedroom to your office, a 10 second walk, and the fact that you can spend more time with your spouse and children, there are other benefits to owning your own business. Please check with your accountant for the complete list, but some of the highlights are: you can write off part of your mortgage payments if you are using part of your house as an office, and only an office. The cost of office supplies, gasoline, postage, etc., if used in conjunction with running your business, will also be a legitimate deduction. The miles that you drive in your business can be written off. If you are traveling domestically or abroad, and part of the trip will be devoted to business, then you can write off most, if not all of the trip as a legitimate business deduction. Check with your accountant **before going,** so that you know not only which items you can deduct, but also what documentation (receipts, photos, business cards, etc.) will be required by the IRS to prove your expenses.

CREDIT CARD MERCHANT ACCOUNT

What is a Credit Card Merchant Account? A CCMA will allow your business to accept Visa, Master Card, Discover (we will deal with American Express in a second). Once your business is up and running and you have steady business, contact your bank and ask them if you can open a merchant account with them. If they do have merchant accounts, go ahead and apply. If they don't have merchant accounts, then ask them for any recommendations that they might have for other banks who offer merchant accounts for small to medium size businesses like yours. When you obtain a merchant account, do not forget that the percentage you will pay for the privilege of accepting credit cards is negotiable. (By that we mean, they may tell you they will charge you 5% on all the transactions that go through your merchant account, tell them that your average ticket price will be a good amount, ie. above $50 or that you will be doing a large volume in credit card charges, and you should be able to negotiate a rate between 2% and 3%.)

If you cannot find a bank that will give you a merchant account, contact your local Chamber of Commerce or ask your bank if they know of any companies who will allow you to run credit charges through them. There are several companies that provide this service.

Why should you go to all this effort to accept credit cards? If you are looking to expand your business or increase the number of your sales, then credit cards will enable you to do both. This may not be important in the early stages of your business but will become more important as your business grows. When you do have a merchant account set up and you deposit your credit card charges (or electronically deposit credit card charges) these funds will be in your account within 24-48 hours.

American Express...once you have a Visa or Master Card merchant account, getting set up with American Express to accept their card is easy. Contact American Express directly (look in the phone book for their nearest office). American Express is very willing to help small businesses in their efforts to accept AE cards. When you are an AE merchant account, you will mail your AE charge tickets directly to them and the percentage you will pay them is determined solely by how quickly you want your money back. Account rates vary from 5% downward...the quicker you want your money back, the higher the charge. Unless you are a large company or are doing a very large volume, they are not usually negotiable on these rates.

In summary, there may be several things that you must do to set up your business, but do not let the bureaucratic red tape get you down and prevent you from starting your business. Organize what you need to do to get going (ie. get your DBA, sales tax number, open a bank account, etc. in a day or two.) **Don't let anything stop you! CONCENTRATE ON THE IMPORTANT THING........**

STARTING YOUR BUSINESS !!!

ADVERTISING

AND

MARKETING

YOUR NEW BUSINESS

ADVERTISING AND MARKETING
YOUR NEW BUSINESS

This section is designed to help you not only get your new business started but to give you ideas on how to expand your new business in the years to come.

Many of the ideas that we will suggest to you will not only be highly effective but also inexpensive. This is very important as keeping your overhead low in the early days (and even when you're well established) is extremely important. The main reason for this is that you are in business to MAKE money, and the lower you keep your costs, the better chance (and the more time) you have to succeed.

An important thing for you to know and remember: usually your first series of ads will not necessarily produce a great number of new customers or orders. Most customers will have to see your ad several times before noticing it and taking action. So what we are trying to say is...advertising is essential to your business but your results will improve with continued advertising over the long haul. (Even when you are successful, you will still need to advertise. Look at McDonalds!)

Bulletin Boards: you will find these to be very inexpensive (usually free) and an effective way to advertise your business. When you place your ads on a bulletin board, you advertise directly in the local market that you wish to serve. You can also increase the effectiveness of this type of ad by giving a special offer eg. buy one get one free, half off, etc. (tell your customers that they must mention that they saw your ad on the bulletin board in order to get the discount.)

That way, you will know where your business is coming from, and which ad, at which location, is most effective. Bulletin boards can be found at supermarkets, places of worship, schools, restaurants, specialty stores, gyms, etc.

Local Newspapers: your local newspaper will offer you two main advantages. First, your ad will be seen by thousands of potential customers in the exact market you will be serving. Secondly, the cost of your ad will be fairly inexpensive (ask if they have any specials such as pay for two weeks-get one week free. Do not be afraid to negotiate for a lower price for your ad). To increase the response of your ad, include a discounted offer such as buy one-get one free, and place a dotted line border around the coupon so that they have to cut it out. This will allow you to see how well your ad is doing.

Flyers: you can have a thousand or more flyers printed up at your local office supply store for under $10. Then either you can distribute them yourself or you can pay your child or a local high school student to distribute them.

The best places to pass out your flyers will depend on your business. Example: if you are selling nutritional foods, place the flyers on cars outside of gyms. Other good locations would be supermarkets, theaters, sporting arenas, flea markets, etc.

You can also deliver them directly to houses in your neighborhood. Do not put them in mailboxes. This is against postal regulations. Instead, put them on doors or on cars. We recommend that you don't do this on a windy day.

To make your flyer most effective, try to be creative or add some humor (you can see examples of this through our book with the use of "clip art"...drawings or cartoons. Clip Art is the name of a type of book that is available from your local bookstore and contains drawings/cartoons that you can cut out, paste on your flyers and then copy.) Once again, include a discount on your flyer eg. two for one, half off, etc. This should increase response from your flyers and by putting a place for their name and address, you can see which neighborhoods are most interested in your product or service. At the same time, by keeping their name and address, you have a mailing list for future offers.

Business Cards: your business cards should clearly state exactly what your business is, including your phone number, an address, and your name or the name of your business. This will be one of your cheapest forms of advertising, so by clearly stating the type of business that you have, it will help market your business. Hand these out to EVERYONE! Place them on bulletin boards/notice boards, leave them in restaurants...just get them OUT!
One clever way of using your business card is to go to a major office supply store and purchase self-adhesive magnetic backs to which you can stick your business cards. Voila! ... **instant REFRIGERATOR MAGNETS!** When we last checked, they were about $20 for 100 magnetic backs. (In the beginning, just use these for your regular customers. If you want to use these in large numbers, contact a business novelty item manufacturer.)

City and National Newspapers: when you are ready to expand, or you believe the product will sell to a larger market, or you wish to include mail order as part of your business, then city and national newspapers will help you increase your market.

Classified ads will be less expensive than space ads. (Classified ads are small ads usually found in the classified section.) If your headline is well worded, and reaches your potential customers, with a good/interesting offer, then it is possible to get good results with a classified ad

Space ads (ie. these ads range in size from 1" by 1" to full page ads) will usually produce greater sales than classified ads but cost a lot more! If you decide to use these, find out from the newspaper what types of people read their paper to make sure you have enough potential customer for your product or service.

The newspaper will usually offer to help create your ad, however, keep in mind that their main goal is to sell you as big an ad as possible. We recommend that you create your own ad. This includes a strong headline, a complete description of your product/service (complete but in as few words as possible), offers a discount with an expiration date, states how to order and methods of payment that you accept.

Radio: if you decided to advertise on the radio, you will need to find a station whose listeners are most likely to be potential customers. (Example: if you are selling beef jerky, a country and western station would most likely be a good bet.)

The radio station will usually help you create your ad ("spot"). Make sure that your product or service is clearly described in your "spot" and that the radio station does not just create a catchy ad that sounds good but does not sell your product/service. (Many stations will produce "your message" for free when you buy a certain number of "spots".)

Radio ads can be fairly inexpensive especially when you negotiate a better price by: accepting "slots" at odd times of the day or negotiating for reduced rates if you buy more "spots". Also ask them about **"unsold"** "spots" (these are advertising time slots that the radio station has already included in their programming but has not sold).

Tip: ask to have your "spot" run first when the music stops. The reason for this is that most people change stations when the ads start to run but they usually hear the first ad.

TV/Cable: TV advertising works, and works very well. So when and if you believe you are ready to try and dramatically increase your business, then advertising via TV or Cable could be the way for you to go. Keep in mind that this will be more expensive than any other form of advertising that you have done in the past. Not only will you have to pay for the advertising space, but you will also have to pay for the cost of filming your ad (however, some stations and cable companies will produce this for you inexpensively or free). Usually cable advertising is less expensive and can be run in a selected area, in or around your business location.

Your ad can run anywhere from 15 seconds to 2 minutes and will cost accordingly. One way to obtain cheaper ads is to buy packages from your local station or cable company that will include a few good spots (good times of the day, or when good shows are on) and a lot more "so so" spots (your ad will appear late at night, early in the morning, and wherever the station needs a filler.)   But this package will enable you to place inexpensive ads on TV as low as $20-$50 per ad based on a package price of "X" number of ads for "X" number of dollars. (This price may or may not include the cost of producing your ad.)   If your sales improve from this type of advertising, then you can increase the number and quality of your ads.

Leg Work: when you first start your business, and even further on down the road, this is the cheapest form of marketing, and the most direct. What does leg work mean? This approach is most effective if you are planning on selling your product wholesale.   You will personally be calling on prospective buyers (eg. restaurants, gourmet shops, gifts stores, specialty stores, and buyers for supermarkets, chain stores, department stores, etc.) and personally presenting and selling your products to them.

You have two choices using this approach. First, when dealing with stores and businesses owned by individuals, you can go directly to their place of business, ask to speak to them personally, and present your product or service, giving them samples, if appropriate.   Then you will try and convince them of the value of your product/service and show them how it will benefit their business (example: higher profit margin, uniqueness, supplying a product that their customers need and will buy, etc.) Secondly, when you are trying to sell to supermarkets, department stores, chain stores, and absent business owners, you will first need to phone whoever is in charge of buying. Explain your business or service to them, tell them how you believe your product/service will benefit their business and ask for an appointment to demonstrate your product/service. Or if it's more appropriate or convenient, arrange to send a sample of your product to them and tell them you will phone a few days later and see what they thought about your product. **Be certain to call them** a day or two after they have received your product.

Word Of Mouth: this is by far the best form of advertising you can ever receive! In order for you to receive GOOD word of mouth advertising, always, ALWAYS, **ALWAYS,** give your customers GREAT service and FRIENDLY service. By paying attention to details, giving quality products and service, and occasionally (or always) giving your customer more than they expect, or pay for, you will build a loyal base of customers. These customers will consistently use your business and, by word of mouth, recommend you to their friends and acquaintances, thereby greatly increasing your business.

Computer Bulletin Boards: this is a new and growing avenue to advertise your products or services. There are many computer bulletin boards, some general and some very specialized. If you have a computer, or know someone who has a computer, then you can access and advertise on these bulletin boards.

Because this is a new field, we are still learning about it ourselves. Therefore we recommend that if you are interested in advertising on these, that you research them carefully yourself (there are many books available in your local bookstore or library). Or if you know someone who is very familiar with these, pick their brains for information.

We believe this avenue has great potential now and down the road, and if it is of interest to you, we encourage you to pursue it.

Coupons: when you are in business, you will find that there are many companies that are producing coupon books and doing coupon mail outs.   Plus, many businesses reduce the cost of certain items by including ads from other businesses (examples: supermarket checkout receipts, bowling alley score sheets, high school sporting programs, etc.) If by using any of the above mentioned coupons, you believe you can reach potential customers, inexpensively and effectively, then do so. Once again, include a discount offer that requires them to bring in the coupon, so that you can see which coupons produce the best results for your business.

Magazines: if your product is in a very clearly defined market (eg. dehydrated foods would be good in magazines devoted to hikers, survivalists or health food addicts, etc.), then advertising in a specialty magazine would be a very good way to sell your product to thousands of people who are definitely interested in your product. This approach works best for mail order. If you are selling just one product, describe it clearly, including price and method of payment, and have them order directly. If you have many items, give them a brief description and have them request a catalog from you, unless of course you want to spend more money on a larger ad.

One of your considerations when advertising in magazines is that you will usually have to wait at least 30 days before your ad will appear (this is referred to as "lead time") but you will have to pay for the ad when you place it. When you continue to advertise in the same magazines, you can usually arrange to be billed for your ads at a later date. (One plus for magazine ads...because people keep their magazines for long periods of time, you will receive orders long after your ad has first appeared.)

Flea Markets/Swap Meets: by renting a booth, this not only gives you the opportunity to sell your products or service at retail but you can also advertise for wholesale accounts at the same time. Plus, you can ask people who buy from you if they wish to be put on your mailing list. You can then inform them of upcoming sales, new products that you are selling, and remind them of holidays and special occasions that would be suitable for your product or service. If you subsequently open a store, by contacting customers on your mailing list, you will have potential customers from day one. (If you decide that you would rather just do mail order, then you already have a customer list.)

One additional idea: by setting up in a flea market/swap meet, you can test market your product or service, quickly and inexpensively. Ask people for their honest opinions of your product or service, good or bad. This will help you make any changes that you think are necessary to improve your business. (We suggest you use 3x5 cards so that they can write down their opinions and place them in a box. By writing their opinions, you are more likely to get an honest opinion.)

Fairs: most large cities and towns have either a state or local fair, one or more times a year. If you have a product that sells well, here is an opportunity to make a large amount of money in a short period of time. The reason being, most people go to fairs to have a good time and spend money. What this means for you is that your product will be seen by a large number of eager BUYERS.

You will find it a lot easier to get into a fair if you have a very unique product or at least a product that is not already being sold there. Once you get into a fair, that is when the work begins. You will usually have to build your own booth (some fairs supply or rent these). Then the fun begins! You will be working long hours. But they will be busy, fun and potentially extremely profitable hours! (You can collapse after the fair is over...and count your money!) Example: in the Dallas fair, one man who started selling corny dogs many years ago, only works the 21 days of the fair and makes a very handsome profit from those 21 days. ie. He doesn't have to work the rest of the year.

You can find a listing of fairs nationwide at your local library. If this appeals to you, you can use the same concept for street festivals, conventions, church outings, in fact anywhere there are large crowds for a short period of time.

Trade Shows: most businesses have a trade show. Your business should be no exception. A trade show is where sellers (ie. YOU) will lease a booth, and display their goods to buyers specifically interested in your product line. This gives you the opportunity to greatly increase your wholesale business in a short amount of time with the added bonus that the buyers come to YOU. Giving away small samples, if appropriate, is a good marketing technique at these shows. (You can reduce the cost of your booth, and other expenses, by selling samples at wholesale prices to individuals who are not placing wholesale orders.)

You can locate these trade shows through publications at your library and by looking in magazines that are geared to your type of business.

Mail Order: mail order is a booming business! It involves selling your product by advertising in print (ie. junk mail, newspapers, magazines, etc.) and asking your customers to order, pay for, and receive your product through the mail. We could write a book describing all the aspects of mail order, but instead you can find many good books at your library or local bookstore that will give you a complete rundown of the mail order business .

Wholesale vs. Retail: for those of you who know the difference between wholesale and retail, you can skip this description.

Simply put, retail is when you are selling your product or service directly to the end user (ie. the customer). You will be selling in smaller amounts to many people and they will be paying full retail price.

Wholesale involves selling larger quantities to other businesses who will in turn wholesale it themselves, or most likely, retail it themselves. When you wholesale, your profit margin will usually be lower but you will make more money because you will be selling in larger quantities. Remember that your wholesale price must be such as to allow YOUR buyer to make a reasonable profit when they in turn, sell.

How will you determine your prices? There are several points that you will have to take into consideration to determine what you will sell your product or service for:

1. How much your product/ service will cost you, including packaging, advertising, delivery and any other overhead.

2. How much time you have put in to making the product or performing the service. (Don't get emotional in pricing the value of your time. Don't under value or over value your efforts to where you price yourself out of the market or sell your time too cheaply.)

3. How much is your competition charging for the exact same product/service (taking into account differences in quality.)

4. If wholesaling, am I leaving enough profit margin in the product to make it profitable for me, yet attractive to the buyer?

5. You can charge a higher profit margin for a luxury or unique items because you will be selling less of them and buyers of luxury items expect to pay more.

6. When selling a non-luxury item, but not quite a basic necessity (ie. everyday foods), you have two choices. You can work on a lower profit margin and sell larger retail quantities or charge slightly more and expect to sell slightly less.

Tip: Remember that it is easier to charge a little more and then come down in price, then it is to charge less and try to raise the price.

WHERE

SHOULD I START

MY

NEW BUSINESS

WHERE SHOULD I START MY NEW BUSINESS

Now that you have decided upon a business, you have several places that you can start your own business. The obvious ones are from your home or from a store; however, throughout this book, we have mentioned numerous other locations from which you, as a budding entrepreneur, can operate. In this chapter we will go through the various locations and discuss the various pros and cons of each.

AT HOME: There are many advantages to operating from your home. The most obvious is the low overhead, reflected in business rent, office utilities, construction/remodeling cost (called "build-out"), and management costs. The only thing that you will need to add, potentially, is some equipment. If you do not have a computer at present, do not feel that you must rush out and purchase one. Even in today's technological age, many business are not computerized. As you grow, you may indeed decide to purchase a computer to streamline your systems, but by waiting until the need truly arises, you will be better able to select the proper computer for your specific requirements, including the all critical, software. In another section of this book, we have included business forms that you can customize with your company name (or your own), address and phone number before taking it to a copy shop.

What you will need is a specific location within you home from which to run your business. This may be a desk complete with a calculator and telephone, or a converted bedroom. You will need to check on the city regulations related to operating a business from your home. In our area, a home business is legal if no sign is posted at curbside and your clients do not visit the location (obviously the intent is to prevent your business from negatively impacting your neighbors, either from excessive parking requirements, or strangers coming into the neighborhood.)

Any other equipment you will need will be determined by the type of business that you decide to start. Many cities have restaurants supply houses but may not sell to you unless you have a business license (or DBA) and business bank account. Don't forget the bargains that are frequently available through auctions of restaurants going out of business. In our area, auctions are listed on the last page of the classified section, Sunday paper.

A Note Of Caution! If you buy at auction, you may or may not really know the condition of the items that you've purchased. This is particularly true of electrical or gas operated equipment such as stoves, refrigerators, kitchen appliances, etc. Some auctions pride themselves on making certain that all equipment in their auction is in working order. Check them out and ask other people whom you meet at the "inspection period", a time set aside prior to the auction for inspection of all items that are slated to be sold. In some instances, the inspection period id held a day or two prior to the auction... in others, it is set several hours prior to commencing the actual bidding. Non mechanical equipment may be a better bet at an auction if you are a auction novice.

Some Tips For Running A Business From Home: A lot of new businesses that operate from home fall into the trap of not setting aside specific time to handle the various aspects of their business. Rather they simply do business when they get to it. they allow anything and everything to interrupt their business efforts and then wonder why their business fails. The business didn't fail...their effort failed. Businesses aren't a hobby...it is a BUSINESS and must be treated as such. You must set aside specific hours in which to operate your business and inform your family that, unless it is an emergency, you are not to be interrupted. If you don't set specific times to run your business, you will find that your energies are diverted to household chores, unrelated telephone calls/chats with friends, playing with the children, picking up the clothes in a room that you pass through, cleaning up the kitchen when you intended to simply get a cup of coffee... but not doing the business chores. Many mothers have stated that one of the benefits of a home based business is getting to spend time with their children. TRUE! But allocate "specific" time, rather than "any ole time that your children want your attention." You will become frustrated and early success will allude you.

Set up a business bank account, even if it only has $50 to $100 dollar in it to start. This will encourage you to keep your household money separate from your business funds and will make tax time much easier. This does not mean that, with profits mounting and checks being deposited into the business account, that you can't take money out for yourself, It does mean that you should write yourself a pay check and deposit it into your personal account to pay "personal bills". "PERSONAL" is personal. "BUSINESS" is business. Remember to set aside money to pay your income tax. A saving account is an excellent way to have money when the time comes to meet with your tax preparer. Ask what percent of your income you should deposit into this account and do not touch it for any other purposes. Having to take out a loan to pay your taxes isn't a wise move, except in a true emergency situation.

FLEA MARKETS/SWAP MEETS: Flea markets are easy to locate. The easiest way to locate them is to look in the phone book under flea markets or swap meets or simply talk to your friends and they will probably know how to help you. The cost of setting up at a flea market will vary, determined by the size of the flea market and the attendance each weekend. Once you have located several flea markets we recommend that you visit several over a weekend to select the one that is most appropriate for your business. You are looking for several things: how many people are attending (and buying!), notice whether the people are carrying shopping bags or packages (more packages=more buyers rather than lookers). This will also help you determine if the price that the flea market is charging for your booth will be a good investment for you specific business.

Ask what equipment the management supplies, ie. tables, chairs, canopies, electricity, etc. The less equipment they supply, the more you will have to supply. Picnic tables and chairs are easily transported but make sure that your equipment will support the weight of your products. do not have a table that is either too large or small for your products. Consider how you will display the products for maximum impact on your potential buyers. do not forget a canopy of some sort, even if it is just a tarpaulin stretched between some poles...necessary for both sun and rain.

Ask if you will be able to keep your vehicle at your display area or are required to park it elsewhere in which case you may need to purchase a "dolly" with which to transport your products and display equipment.

Find out what hours the flea market is open and determine if you can handle these hours or need help from friends or relatives or need to hire someone to help you. You need to include all of these expenses and considerations in determining if this is the best location for your specific business.

Some Tips For Running A Business From A Flea Market/Swap Meet: When you have decided which flea market/swap meet to set in, you should plan to use this location at least 3 to 4 times. This will enable you to determine if this particular flea market/swap meet will permit you to generate sufficient sales each weekend to make your business profitable. Ask other vendors at the flea market if this is the best season or if other seasons (or months) are better for sales. If they confirm that this month is not the best, consider waiting until a better month to begin your sales, giving your business a "quick start" to success. Ask them if they participate in other locations as well (they may have more than one booth) and which flea market/swap meet they prefer. Be ready to negotiate with buyers as this is what they are accustomed to at flea markets and swap meets.

STREET FESTIVALS: You can find street festivals by contacting the Chamber of Commerce in your town and surrounding communities and ask what festivals they have scheduled in upcoming months. Most cities have at least one or two with some cities having substantially more than that.

Get the name, address and telephone number for the organizer. Contact them as soon as possible because good street festivals usually sell their booth very early. Determine if they will have booths, if they are sold out, and if not, how much the booth will cost (most booths are 10'x10' or are charged in increments of 10'x10' so decide how much space you really need). Ask how many people attended last year and the previous year and use this information to determine if there will be enough market for your products or service to warrant spending the money for a booth.

Some Tips For Running A Business From A Street Festival: Most street festivals do not supply any equipment so you will have to provide your own tables and clothes, chairs, canopy, etc. (We recommend strongly that if you live in a sunny area or anticipate the possibility of rain, plan to have a canopy of some sort, even if you make it yourself...it beats being burned to a crisp or getting drenched.)

Ask the following questions: does the street festival charge for admittance, what hours is it open, how much advance advertising do they do, how many other vendors are selling the same or similar products/services (the less competition, in general, the more sales for you.)

TRADE SHOWS: The best place to locate trade shows is to contact both the trade organizations or trade magazines devoted to your specific area of business. When you contact them, ask for dates, locations and the name, address and telephone number of the organizer (person or persons in charge of planning the event.) Contact them as rapidly as possible because trade show booths fill up quickly, frequently by past year participants. The good things about trade shows is that people are there to purchase items in specific areas, such as yours, frequently in large quantities. You can also go into trade shows that aren't specifically tailored to your market if you think that buyers at the show will be prone to consider your product/service too. (ie. jewelry might be a winning item at a show that is attended primarily by women, even though jewelry might have nothing to do with the specific area of interest at the trade show.)

Determine the cost of the booth, what equipment is supplied, where you must enter when bringing in your product, etc. Ask if you must supply any lights as most trade shows are held indoors. Look at the attendance figures for last year and the prior year to help you determine if this is a good expenditure for you. Are attendees charged an admittance fee? What are the trade show hours (determine if you need assistance) and during what hours are you allowed to set up. Check out their advance advertising. Who has the right to attend...the general public, only wholesale buyers or both?

Some Tips For Running A Business From A Trade Show: A good thing to have at trade shows is business cards. Give them to everyone. Also make certain that you collect business cards from anyone who shows an interest in your product/service. Follow-up after the show is over by sending each person (or company) a brochure or flyer and a thank you note. Two weeks after you have mailed the flyer, call to see if they have any questions and ask if they would like to place an order.

Be prepared to take orders at the Trade Show. See the "forms" section for further assistance.

CONVENTIONS: Locate conventions through the convention bureau in your city (it may be named the convention and visitors bureau, etc. The information operator usually knows what name to check.) If you are really gung-ho, you can also check with some of the larger hotels to see if they are hosting conventions or trade shows, many of which are not known by the convention bureau. Contact the organizer and follow the guidelines as listed above. Because the participants are there for a number of days, the BUY!

BUSINESS

AND

ADVERTISING

DOCUMENTS

BUSINESS AND ADVERTISING DOCUMENTS

There are some basic documents that will ease your way into the new business that you've decided to pursue. We have attached copies of the following in APPENDIX I:

1) Purchase Order: customize this form with your name (or company name), address and phone number in the upper right corner. If you have a fax, add the number. If not, locate a business that will accept your faxes (usually a local copy shop, stationers or mail box center and include their number. Many business won't take you seriously if you don't have a fax machine available. This form should be used when YOU place an order and when others are ordering from you and do not have their own purchase order form.

2) Invoice: use this form to invoice wholesale customers. It can also be used for retail customers who order product. Other forms are available at local stationers. It is customized in the same way as Purchase Order.

3) Weekly Planner: helpful for keeping track of meetings, trade shows, dates to prepare and mail invoices, dates for placing orders yourself, etc. It will also make your accountant very happy if you also record your expenses.

4) Quarterly Cash Flow: use this to track the success of your business. Rejoice and do something special for yourself each time that a quarter proves to be more successful that the last. If a quarter dips, don't panic. Analyze what you can improve on and then get into action!

5) Mileage Record: also designed to keep your accountant (and more importantly the IRS) happy. Customize it in the upper right hand corner.

6) Application For Employment: should you decide to hire employees, here is a form for that purpose.

7) Advertising Blanks: we have included 8 variations blanks that can be customized for advertising, flyers, sales, announcements, etc.

This should give you a good basic start toward organizing your business, right from the beginning.

BUSINESS

OPPORTUNITIES

BARBECUE COOK

Description Of Opportunity: You will be cooking and selling barbecue direct to the public as well as other food items such as potato salad, cole slaw, baked potato, corn, cookies, brownies, chips, drinks, and beer (if you can get a license and it is suitable for the location in which you are setting up. eg. It would not be suitable if you are catering a church social.)

How Much Money To Start? $200 to $3,000 plus

Equipment Needed: You have two choices. Part-time cooks will need a trailer with a barbecue pit that you can either buy new, build yourself or buy used from someone who is going out of business. You will need signs listing the food items that you sell including prices. Disposal plates, knives, forks. Coolers for drinks and cooking supplies. Hickory (or other) wood for barbecuing and a reliable vehicle. If you wish to do this full time, in a permanent location, you'll need a good on-site barbecue pit, benches and a covered area for people to sit and eat. Also signs, advertising your business and location so people can see and find your business.

Can Opportunity Be Operated From Home? Yes & No
Yes if it's part time, no if you are full-time.

How Quickly Can It Be Up & Running? As little as 1 week.

Special Skills Or Knowledge: You definitely need some great recipes and good barbecue sauce. You will need to check with your Health Department for the appropriate licenses and health requirements for both temporary and permanent food businesses.

Starting Your Business: For you part-time cooks, locate flea markets, street festivals, conventions, auctions, fairs, company picnics, and church dinners. You can do this through your library, local paper, or simply asking people at other shows or events for information on other upcoming events.

With auctions, you can contract with an auctioneer who has regular sales, to set up and sell food, possibly paying him a small fee.   Flea markets give you the opportunity to earn a regular income without having to be in a full-time business.

For the full-time barbecue cooks, you have several choices. You can either operate from your land, if you are on, or close to, a busy thoroughfare, or lease (or lease with an option to buy) some land, near a busy street. You will have to check with your local planning office to see if the property, you wish to operate your barbecue business on, is zoned for commercial business. Next build a barbecue pit or you can use your portable pit. You will need to furnish tables and chairs, a covered area and a sign advertising your location.   When your business takes off you can decide if you want to expand by building a permanent restaurant.

A good way to expand your business is to use 2 for 1 coupons, punch cards (buy 10 meals, get 11th free), discount coupons, and give low prices for childrens meals. By giving low prices for kids meals you will be bringing in the whole family.

HEALTHY BREADS AND DESSERTS

Description Of Opportunity: You will be filling a growing market need, namely, a demand for low fat, low sodium, breads, cakes, brownies, cookies, etc.

How Much Money To Start? $100 and up

Equipment Needed: Mixer, bread and dessert molds, boxes and other packaging materials.

Can Opportunity Be Operated From Home? Yes

How Quickly Can It Be Up & Running? Within 1 week

Special Skills Or Knowledge: You will need healthy, low or no fat recipes for breads and several desserts, including my favorite, chocolate anything! If you don't have any good recipes, you can find many great cookbooks at the library and bookstores. Check with your Health Department to see if you need any licenses for running this business out of your home.

Starting Your Business: Contact businesses that cater to health conscious consumers of businesses that sells food items, such as health food stores, gyms, Mom & Pop stores, convenience stores, chiropractors, supermarkets. Tell them about your unique and healthful products. Supply them with samples. Take orders and enjoy the sweet and healthy taste of success.

TEACH COOKING

Description Of Opportunity: There are many people out there who don't know how to cook ANYTHING, or if they can cook, have a limited range of recipes. These people include new brides, bachelors, housewives, senior citizens, and individuals who love different foods but have no idea how to prepare them.

This is where you come in. If you love to cook and have the patience to teach, enjoy people, and are organized, then this business may be perfect for you.

How Much Money To Start? Under $100

Equipment Needed: Items from your own kitchen such as pots, pans, cutlery, plates, bowls, seasonings, and food items required for your recipes.

Can Opportunity Be Operated From Home? Yes

How Quickly Can It Be Up & Running? Immediately

Special Skills Or Knowledge: You must really be a great cook! With the talent to cook a variety of things, from simple basic foods to gourmet meals, ethnic dishes, or regional dishes.

Starting Your Business: You can either have classes in your home or in the home of your students. The best way to advertise your service is through local newspaper ads, supermarket and church bulletin boards, local bride directories or bridal shops, senior citizens centers, PTA/PTO organizations, gourmet or ethnic food stores, local activity magazines. You also have the option to offer this service at an adult education center or your local "Y". One advantage to this approach is that they do the advertising for you. A possible disadvantage is that you will only get a portion of the fees that your students pay.

SELL SEAWEED

Description Of Opportunity: You will be collecting, drying, and then grinding seaweed to a powder or leaving it intact, for immediate consumption. At that point, you can either package it for individual or bulk sale. (Many people eat seaweed in salads, soups, health shakes, sushi, and even in baby formulas.)

How Much Money To Start? As little as nothing.

Equipment Needed: Collection bags, a convenient ocean, packaging material and labels.

Can Opportunity Be Operated From Home? Yes if you live near the coast.

How Quickly Can It Be Up & Running? Today!

Special Skills Or Knowledge: You must have (or acquire) a knowledge of edible seaweeds (knowing vitamins and trace minerals that are present in seaweed is not necessary but would be helpful in your marketing efforts.) A good reference book is "Seaweeds and Their Uses" by V.J.Chapman.

Starting Your Business: You will be marketing this product to health food stores, supermarkets that specialize in natural foods or ethnic foods (eg. Japanese cooking), or supermarkets that have a natural foods section. You can also market it directly to the public through health food and natural food catalogs. (Seaweed has a long shelf-life and therefore is ideal for mail order sales.)

MUSHROOM FARMER

Description Of Opportunity: A whole variety of mushrooms are in constant demand from various restaurants and other businesses. You can grow any variety, from button mushrooms to rare and exotic mushrooms. This can easily be determined by asking businesses what variety of mushrooms they require and in what quantities.

How Much Money To Start? From $100 and up

Equipment Needed: A dark, ventilated, room. Mushroom spawn, rich soil. High quality fertilizer, potting trays. Packaging materials.

Can Opportunity Be Operated From Home? Yes

How Quickly Can It Be Up & Running?
Approximately 1 month

Special Skills Or Knowledge: If you don't have knowledge of our little fungi friends, this can easily be corrected by borrowing books on growing mushrooms from your library, or purchasing a book (or books) on mushroom growing. For example, "Mushroom Growing" by Arthur Simons.

Starting Your Business: As we stated, numerous businesses constantly require mushrooms: restaurants, health food stores, supermarkets, gourmet stores, caterers, salad restaurants, buffet restaurants. You can make personal contact with these businesses . or phone them, informing them of the variety of mushrooms you are (or will be) growing and the prices per pound and take orders for now and in the future.

Here are two ways to increase your business: first, ask your customers what other varieties of mushrooms they would buy if you were growing them, and in what quantity, so you can see if it would be worth your while to grow them! Secondly, you can expand the number of your customers by supplying similar businesses in surrounding cities and towns.

HERB RANCHER

Description Of Opportunity: Fresh herbs, grown naturally without harmful chemicals, will always have a market, both for individual and commercial use. Herbs are easy to grow, indoors or out, in all seasons and conditions. They require very low maintenance and are easy to "round up" when it's harvesting time!

How Much Money To Start? As little as $100

Equipment Needed: Herb starter packs, good soil, and fertilizer, and packaging materials.

Can Opportunity Be Operated From Home? Yes

How Quickly Can It Be Up & Running? Within 1-2 months

Special Skills Or Knowledge: It would be helpful to know which herbs sell well, and at a price that makes them profitable to grow.

Starting Your Business: This is a very easy business to start. You can purchase your seeds, which come with directions on growing them, at garden centers, nurseries and via mail order companies. Once you have planted a good quantity and variety of herbs, you will need to market your herbs to the following types of businesses: restaurants, health food stores, supermarkets, specialty and gourmet stores, and at farmers markets. You can also package your herbs and sell them via mail order by advertising in a variety of publications: food and cooking magazines, health and fitness magazines.

SELLING FOOD ITEMS AT FARMERS MARKETS OR ROADSIDE STANDS

Description Of Opportunity: You can sell a whole variety of food items at either location: fruits, vegetables, herbs, mushrooms, cakes, pies, candies, desserts, honey, jams, preserves, dehydrated food items, crafts, specialty and weird foods, such as quail, frozen buffalo meat, rattlesnake steak, rabbits (got the idea??)

How Much Money To Start? From $100 and up

Equipment Needed: If you decide to set up a roadside stand, you will need anything from a large umbrella to a permanent structure. As for a Farmers Market, many of them already have some kind of cover. If this is the case at your local Farmers Market, all well and good. If not, you may need to put up a large umbrella or make a canopy, using a tarpaulin, canvas, or purchase a pre-packaged canopy (check with your local camping or outdoors store.)

You will also need some tables and chairs. An attractive way to display your food items...ie. small baskets, wooden trays, etc. You will also need some bags and boxes for your customers. Also include larger boxes and coolers to carry and store your food items.

Can Opportunity Be Operated From Home? Yes

How Quickly Can It Be Up & Running? Within a week

Special Skills Or Knowledge: You will need to know how to make pies, cakes, and cookies. Preserve fruits or vegetables. Make honey, etc. The more items you know how to make, the more you can sell year round.

Starting Your Business: If you live in the country, simply set up a road side stand on your land, or lease some land nearby. Be sure that you are on a well traveled road and you have room for the cars to stop and park. If you live in the city, or live in the country and want more business, locate a farmers market and pay a small fee to set up and sell your produce and products.

P.S. Don't miss a potential market (ie. when someone buys an item from you, ask them if they would like to be added to your mail order list.) This enables you to start your own mail order business with your preserves, honey, pies, fruits, etc.   This will give you the opportunity to sell a lot more of your food items around holiday times, such as Thanksgiving and Christmas. (Be sure to tell your customers to order early for the BIG holiday, to give you time to prepare for them.)

ORGANIC GARDENER

Description Of Opportunity: You will be growing fruits, vegetables, herbs, and edible flowers in a natural, organic environment,   instead of using potentially harmful chemicals and pesticides.

How Much Money To Start? $200 plus

Equipment Needed: You will need to begin with seeds or plant starters that have been raised in organic soil.   Your own land or back yard or leased land. Gardening tools.   A compost pile.   Rain and Sun.

Can Opportunity Be Operated From Home? Yes

How Quickly Can It Be Up & Running? 2 weeks to several months, depending upon the crops that you've planted.

Special Skills Or Knowledge: You will have to learn how to reduce the bug population naturally.   Jerry Baker has a series of books on Natural Gardening as do Rodale Publishers.   Best times and conditions to plant various crops.   How to start a compost pile. You can get a starter kit at many garden centers.   A green thumb won't hurt!

Starting Your Business: You have a whole host of potential customers, including your family, friends, and neighbors.   Restaurants,   health   food   stores, supermarkets, gourmet/specialty stores, caterers, etc. will be eager to buy your organically grown produce to fill their customers. You should have no trouble getting orders once you contact these businesses and inform them about your naturally grown products.

Quick tip: a good portion of your crop should have a short growing cycle and be in demand year round. (eg. tomatoes.) Also check with restaurants, particularly gourmet restaurants, and ask what produce they would like you to add and what quantities they would order, if you were to grow it. This will help you decide how to expand your business profitably, and pre-sell your new crops.

FOOD BASKETS

Description Of Opportunity: You will need to find food wholesalers who carry such things as imported cheese, coffees, teas, honeys, jellies/jams, seasonings, fruit cakes, small bottles of wine/liquor, specialty meats, in fact, any food items that you feel will look good packaged together. Of course, you can pack specific food selections for food lovers, eg. chocolate lovers, coffee lovers, cheese lovers, or specialty items reflecting your state. All you need to do next is package them attractively with synthetic straw or any other decorative material. Then wrap the total package in cellophane.

How Much Money To Start? $200 plus

Equipment Needed: You will need to find an attractive line of gift baskets. You can do this by checking with importers in the Yellow Pages, or in your local craft or plant stores. You will need cellophane for the outer wrapping and synthetic straw and glitter for decorating the inside of the basket.

Can Opportunity Be Operated From Home? Yes

How Quickly Can It Be Up & Running? Within 1 week

Special Skills Or Knowledge: None

Starting Your Business: After you have found all the needed supplies, assemble several gift baskets and sell them directly by taking them to businesses that will use them as promotional items/gifts such as real estate offices, new home builders, car dealers, etc.

Additionally you can sell them at flea markets, crafts shows, conventions, etc.

However, if you would like to wholesale them and sell larger quantities but with a lower profit margin, you can take them to the following businesses: hotels, gift shops, hospital gift shops, gourmet shops, drug stores, resorts, in fact, anywhere people shop for gifts and/or food.

BE A CHEESECAKE (MAKER)

Description Of Opportunity: Many restaurants, delis, coffee shops, gourmet shops, and pie shops, either do not make their own cheesecakes or make mediocre ones. In fact, many of these businesses buy cheesecakes from home bakers, so if you offer them a great cheesecake, you can literally eat into the competitions profits.

How Much Money To Start? $100

Equipment Needed: You will need a good mixer, springform pans (the side of these pans have a hinge which you can unlatch when the cake is ready), and boxes for delivery.

Can Opportunity Be Operated From Home? Yes

How Quickly Can It Be Up & Running? Immediately

Special Skills Or Knowledge: A great cheesecake recipe. If you don't have one, ask a family member or friend who has a great recipe, if you can use it. Or experiment with recipes in cookbooks till you find a winner.

Starting Your Business: With several cheesecakes in hand, you can call and make appointments with the managers of these businesses and allow them to taste your cheesecakes for themselves. If they love your samples, sign a contract for "x" number of cheesecakes per week per location at a specific price. Before you know it, you will supplying lots of different businesses and will most likely need help in the kitchen. Don't forget your neighbors who give dinner parties, caterers, church socials, etc. These potential customers can be reached by ads in local papers and word of mouth.

Two simple ways to increase the size of your business: first, bake different kinds of cheesecakes eg. white chocolate amaretto, strawberry cheesecake, chocolate cheesecake, etc., etc. Secondly, there is no reason that you can't expand this business with specialty cakes, such as German Chocolate Cake, Black Forest Cake, etc. Or if you prefer, make specialty cakes instead of cheesecakes.

TEMPORARY FOOD BOOTHS

Description Of Opportunity: There are many opportunities to sell food on a part-time basis at many temporary shows and events, and make a full-time income. This can be done from a food trailer, portable kiosk, or food cart.

There are many types of food that you can successfully sell in this way including: hamburgers, hot dogs, Chinese food, fajitas, Mexican food, turkey legs, french fries, corny dogs, ice cream, etc. Don't forget to sell drinks for additional profits.

How Much Money To Start? $500 to over $10,000

Equipment Needed: You will either have to lease, buy or build a booth. You will need cooking equipment, coolers or a refrigerator, drink dispensers, disposable plates, knives & forks, and a price list. All these items can be found at a restaurant supply house.

Can Opportunity Be Operated From Home? Yes/No

How Quickly Can It Be Up & Running? Within 1 month

Special Skills Or Knowledge: You will need to check with your local Health Department for licenses and regulations. You must be able to prepare food in tight spaces and unusual locations.

Starting Your Business: You can find many locations for this type of business. Your main concern should be finding a location where there are lots of people eg. fairs, flea markets, street festivals, conventions, trade shows, auctions, horse races, malls, high school/college sporting events, and other well attended events. As you can see, there are many places available for you to sell food items in your area.

BREAKFAST IN BED SERVICE

Description Of Opportunity: Are you a morning person? Do you like to cook? Do you like meeting new people? Then this might be for you! Lots of people like to be pampered with breakfast in bed but don't like to prepare it themselves. That's where you come in. You will go to your clients home, prepare a complete breakfast with your own cooking equipment and food, display the food attractively on trays, and serve your clients breakfast in bed. Then after a discreet period of time, remove the trays, clean up their kitchen, collect your payment and leave. (Remember to clean your own equipment when you return to your own home, unless you are going to another one of your clients.)

How Much Money To Start? $200 and up

Equipment Needed: Many of these items you'll have in your own kitchen...your pots and pans, plates, bowls, cutlery, glasses, napkins, bed trays, bud vase, and professional clothing (eg. white shirt/blouse, black trousers/skirt) and a reliable vehicle.

Can Opportunity Be Operated From Home? Yes

How Quickly Can It Be Up & Running? Within 1 week

Special Skills Or Knowledge: You should be able to prepare and attractively display a wide selection of breakfast foods and have a friendly personality.

Starting Your Business: In order to get the word out concerning your new business, you will need to advertise in local newspapers, on bulletin boards in supermarkets, places of worship, gyms, "Y's"...in fact anywhere!... after all who doesn't like breakfast in bed!! When people contact you, tell them exactly what you offer, including the choices you offer for breakfast and what your prices are.

Later that day, or the next day, you should definitely phone your customers to make sure they were happy with your service and ask them if they wish to book you on a regular basis. Ask for referrals, and remind them of upcoming holidays, anniversaries and birthdays. Also offer gift certificates so they can give these to their friends and relatives.

FOOD DELIVERY SERVICE

Description Of Opportunity: You will be delivering food from several different restaurants to offices and homes in your area. You will be charging your customers, from $3 to $6 per delivery (tips not included). Your job will be to either answer the phones or have someone else answer them and take the orders. Then call the restaurant and place their order and send your driver to pick up their order and deliver it. Not only can you offer lunch and dinner, but also breakfast. There are several companies already offering this service and doing very well with it, which clearly shows there is a demand for food delivery services.

How Much Money To Start? $200 and up

Equipment Needed: You will need several hot/cold coolers, a menu, a reliable vehicle, and advertising flyers.

Can Opportunity Be Operated From Home? Yes

How Quickly Can It Be Up & Running? Within 1 month

Special Skills Or Knowledge: None

Starting Your Business: You will need to contract several different restaurants in your area and tell them about your business, which will include taking orders for food from their restaurant and several other area restaurants, delivering that order to your customers at their homes or place of work. In exchange, the restaurant will pay you approximately 25% of the price of the food (if you think they won't do this, consider the number of 2 for 1 coupons that restaurants use for advertising that equals 50% off their regular price). Inform the restaurants that you will be copying their menu into your brochure, along with the menus of several other restaurants. If you like, tell them that you will only represent one style of restaurant in your brochure (eg. Chinese, barbecue, etc.) Or you can list several restaurants in each style... the choice is yours. When you pay the restaurants each night, you should have already subtracted your fee. Do not take part of the sales tax! Allow the restaurant to pay this in full. This will save you time when you do your bookkeeping!

CANDY MAKER

Description Of Opportunity: Americans eat a mountain of candy each year! Why let the big companies make all the profits! By creating your own line of candies, you can build a faithful following of "sweet toothed" customers.

How Much Money To Start? $200 and up

Equipment Needed: You will need molds, a good mixer, great recipes, packaging such as boxes and wrappers.

Can Opportunity Be Operated From Home? Yes

How Quickly Can It Be Up & Running? Within 1 week

Special Skills Or Knowledge: You should have several outstanding recipes for different kinds of candies (including a large selection of chocolate ones). Also you will need a flair for packaging, or if you have none, have a friend help you.

Starting Your Business: You will need to test lots of recipes on your families and friends...if you're a good candy maker, you should have plenty of volunteers. Once you have a good selection and variety of candies, make appointments at the following businesses: gourmet shops, theaters, gift stores, flower shops, bakeries, supermarkets, convenience stores, Mom & Pop stores, theme parks, resorts, hotels, hospitals. Let them taste your samples and take their orders. Don't forget special shapes, colors or flavors for holidays such as Easter and Valentines Day. As your business expands, you can add new products to your candy line. For ideas for new products, ask **your** customers for suggestions and for flavors that **their** customers frequently buy or ask for.

CHILDRENS PARTY CATERER

Description Of Opportunity: You will be preparing parties, primarily birthday parties for young children. You must decide how many children you can handle at one time and how many your nerves can handle! You will be supplying everything from tables and chairs, to dishes, food and drinks, depending upon the how you set up your business. You should also offer entertainment.

How Much Money To Start? $200 and up

Equipment Needed: This depends on whether you plan to supply tables, chairs and supplies, including non-disposable utensils and plates/cups or whether you want to only supply disposable plates, forks, spoons, napkins, and allow the hostess to supply everything else.

Can Opportunity Be Operated From Home? Yes

How Quickly Can It Be Up & Running? Within 1 week

Special Skills Or Knowledge: You must like children! A lot!!! You should also have good recipes for birthday cakes, particularly chocolate, and be able to decorate them for children or find a good bakery that will sell to you at a discount. Offer a good selection of healthy, low sodium, low fat foods that taste great so that kids will eat them and their mothers will love them. If you can also entertain by being a clown or magician, you can charge and make even more. (Of course, you can also hire clowns and magicians and include a small fee for yourself in you total bill.)

Starting Your Business: To start your business you will want to advertise to families...local papers, school and supermarket bulletin boards and PTA/PTO newsletters, church newsletters. Some cities have local magazines that highlight activities, schools, and services for children. Place an ad in the Yellow Pages, if you can afford it. Flyers distributed in residential areas work well, as does word of mouth. Always carry business cards with you and hand them out to other parents at the parties you cater.

Always call your host/hostess the next day to see if they liked your work and ask for referrals. Keep track of every family or organization that has hired you including their childrens names and birth dates then send flyers to a former host/hostess about 2 months prior to their childs upcoming birthday. This will help jog their memory about your service. A nice touch is to send a card for each childs birthday. Even if they don't book you for this year, they probably will next time...and they may also tell other people about your business.

CATERING

Description Of Opportunity: You will be catering anything from small gatherings to large formal affairs. Examples might be weddings, bar mitzvahs, company parties, luncheons, graduation parties, company picnics, etc.   You can offer everything from limited service (just food for a small group) to full service including food, furniture, and all the "extras" for a large group.

How Much Money To Start? $500 to several thousand

Equipment Needed: Tables, chairs, linens, including cloth napkins, cutlery, dishes, glasses, pots and pans, and serving dishes, including hot plates ("Salton" trays work wonderfully...they are the flat, glass top trays that plug into an outlet. They look good and keep food hot without re-cooking everything. You can find them at restaurant supply houses.) You may need to provide a means of cooking your food on site.   You can do that with propane cookers.   You will need coolers for hot and cold food.   (It is important to store food properly and at the correct temperature.) You must have a very good, reliable vehicle, such as a van.

Can Opportunity Be Operated From Home? Yes

How Quickly Can It Be Up & Running?   Within 1 month

Special Skills Or Knowledge: You must be able to cook for large groups of people.   The larger selections of foods that you offer, the more jobs you will get. Some ideas: gourmet, barbecue family favorites, ethnic foods. You must be able to organize people as you will additional cooks and waiters/waitresses working for you.

Starting Your Business: Your advertising will depend on whether you want to specialize or take whatever jobs are offered to you. For example, bridal registries, bridal shops and tuxedo rental shops are good if you want to cater wedding receptions. Also read newspapers for announcements of engagements and then contact the bride. If you want to specialize in bar mitzvahs, contact synagogues. To cater graduation parties, contact the high schools and colleges, PTA/PTO and parents groups.

If you want to be a general caterer, advertise in newspapers, on bulletin boards at places of worship, grocery stores, adult centers, etc. The idea is to get your company well known. Build a reputation for giving good service at a fair price. Have a good follow-up program. Call the host/ hostess to make sure they liked the job that you did, ask if they have any other upcoming parties that you might cater. Always ask for referrals, and always carry business cards and have flyers in your vehicle.

Here are some points to consider: How you will prepare the food. Can it be prepared at your home prior to going to the event (be very careful about food storage!). If not, how are you going to cook on site. As you expand, a van equipped with a kitchen or a mobile home with a full kitchen and refrigerator may be a good alternative. They offering a place for storage and a way to transport all of the furniture, dishes, cutlery, pots and pans, serving dishes, etc. that you may require. Remember, however, that there may be times when a two burner hot plate may be all that you need to cater an event. Most of the equipment that you would need to be a caterer is available at restaurant supply stores. If you have no previous experience as a caterer, start small and grow as your knowledge, skills, confidence, and reputation grow! Don't tackle a job that is to big for you when you are just beginning. Better to do a great job of catering on a smaller job and get lots of good will and word of mouth advertising and build up from there.

ARE YOU A FRUIT CAKE?

Description Of Opportunity: You will be making a **good** quality fruitcake to fill all the possible markets for fruitcakes.

How Much Money To Start? $100 plus

Equipment Needed: You will need fruit cake molds, a great recipe, and wrapping material for the finished product. Cellophane works well.

Can Opportunity Be Operated From Home? Yes

How Quickly Can It Be Up & Running? 2-4 weeks

Special Skills Or Knowledge: You will need a really good recipe for fruitcake. Try several! Test them on friends and family and ask for an honest opinion.

Starting Your Business: After you have a great recipe for fruitcakes, contact all of the businesses and organizations that sell them. Grocery stores, bakeries, restaurants, department stores, schools, fund raising groups, gift shops, drug stores, Christmas stores and catalogs, etc. Take or mail samples to them with your price list, minimum order and delivery time and take their orders. You can also increase sales by making fruitcake wedding cakes, fruitcake muffins, etc. By far your largest season for fruitcakes is Christmas. Be prepared to make MANY! Start making fruitcakes before Christmas, so as to have a good supply. For additional profits, sell your fruitcakes by mail order. Start your advertising 1-2 months before Christmas.

MARKET CANDY APPLES

Description Of Opportunity: You will be making candy apples!

How Much Money To Start? $100-300

Equipment Needed: You will need a commercial mixer, wooden sticks, and wrapping material. Cellophane works well. A restaurant supply house is a good source for the mixer and wrapping material.

Can Opportunity Be Operated From Home? Yes

How Quickly Can It Be Up & Running? Within 1 week

Special Skills Or Knowledge: You will need a good recipe for the candy (that will surround the apple.) Don't have one...that's what cookbooks are for. Try several caramel and toffee recipes.

Starting Your Business: You will need to find a good supplier of apples at wholesale prices. Only use first quality apples, ones with no bruises. Once you have perfected the art of making candied apples, you can market them to grocery stores, candy stores, gift stores, hospitals (primarily childrens hospitals), amusement parks, theaters, theme parks, city parks, sports stadiums, daycare centers, etc.

WEDDING CAKE MAKER

Description of Opportunity: Now days, most people buy wedding cakes rather than baking them themselves. If you like to bake, can't or don't like to go out to much, then this would be an ideal business for you. People pay anywhere from $50 to $500 for a good cake. By baking and decorating them at home, you can keep your overhead low.

How Much Money To Start? $100 to $200

Equipment Needed: You will need a commercial mixer, some cake molds, and a supply of boxes for delivery. You will need bride & groom statues, flower tips, pastry bags, etc. to make the flowers and icing decorations.

Can Opportunity Be Operated From Home? Yes

How Quickly Can It Be Up & Running? Immediately

Special Skills or Knowledge: You should have several good cake recipes, from plain to chocolate to cherry cakes and more. You'll need to know how to decorate a cake. If you don't have that skill, there are many places including night schools and bakeries, that offer cake decorating classes.

Starting Your Business: You will need to contact several businesses that deal with weddings: bridal and tuxedo shops, caterers, bridal registries, etc. Inform them that you bake wedding cakes. Advertise on bulletin boards, in local papers, grocery stores, and places of worship. Keep track of the engagement announcements in the local paper and send a letter of congratulations to the bride with your business card and a flyer or brochure enclosed!

Take good photos of each cake that you make, put them into a photo album and use it as your sales catalog. Always send a letter of thanks to the host/hostess, telling them how much you enjoyed helping with the wedding, ask them to keep you in mind for future events (particularly if you also make graduation, birthday, anniversary cakes etc.) and ask them to refer you to their friends.

COFFEE DELIVERY

Description Of Opportunity: If you love coffee, then you know other people are wild about coffee too. By offering individuals and businesses a variety of different coffees, that you will deliver to them, on a daily, weekly or monthly basis, you can build a nice business for yourself. You will need to find a coffee importer or distributor. Check your Yellow Pages. Buying coffee beans in bulk and grinding them at home. Then package them in 1/4, 1/2 and 1 pound packages, and label them as "gourmet coffee" (making sure that you also indicate the flavor). You can also mix and match coffee beans creating your own combinations. Then market them under your own company label.

How Much Money To Start? $200 to $1,000

Equipment Needed: You will need a coffee grinder, some coffee bags with your business name printed on them (or self sticking fancy labels with a space for the name of the coffee eg. French Vanilla) and a scale. These can be purchased at a restaurant supply house.

Can Opportunity Be Operated From Home? Yes

How Quickly Can It Be Up & Running? A couple of days

Special Skills Or Knowledge: None in particular. However, an ability to mix various beans together to make new combinations will be a plus.

Starting Your Business: With samples in hand and more in your car, go to large office buildings and after checking with the owner/office manager, market your coffee to everyone who works there. The best way to do this is to make up samples and let everyone taste your coffee. It would be a good idea to bring a coffee pot with you. When people buy, be sure to give them a flyer and business card. Make certain that you have their name, work and home numbers and their address. Adding them to your customer file and contact them when you are offering new flavors, having a sale or before Christmas.

You can also market your coffee in gourmet shops, gift shops, grocery stores, Mom & Pop stores, convenience stores, mailing stores, hospital gift stores, bakeries, etc. Don't miss the opportunity to market your coffees through the mail as your client list expands. You can even start a coffee of the month club by mailing your coffees to them (and their friends,) in and out of state. Try to establish a regular schedule of deliveries with them...perhaps 2 pounds every six weeks. Be creative in your packaging, allowing your customers to mix and match in 1/2 lb. or 1 lbs. packages, several different varieties of coffee in the same shipment. A good tip: perhaps every third or fourth shipment, include a complimentary sample (enough to make 1 pot of coffee), of a coffee that you would like to introduce to the buyer. It may be one they are already ordering...that's OK...they will enjoying having some extra. If it is one the buyer hasn't ordered before, a sample may be enough for them to include it in their next order. Send the same sample to everyone. Don't try to figure out what coffee a particular buyer hasn't tried before.

SELL BEVERAGES IN VOLUME

Description Of Opportunity: You will be selling sodas in bulk to businesses and to individuals, and then delivering them to your customers. You will be selling the drinks at or below what they would pay at the supermarket, but in volume, at least a case at a time. You can also look into delivering beer, wine and alcohol, but make sure you have checked to determine if you are required to have a license for alcohol deliveries. Also find out if there are restrictions on delivery if you are in a "dry" area. (ie. no alcohol sales in that town or county.)

How Much Money To Start? $200 and up

Equipment Needed: You will need a commercial dolly, a vehicle (van or pickup truck)

Can Opportunity Be Operated From Home? Yes

How Quickly Can It Be Up & Running? Same day

Special Skills Or Knowledge: None

Starting Your Business: Contact soft drink and/or alcohol distributors directly, or manufacturers if they are in your area, eg. Dr. Pepper, Coca Cola, Pepsi, etc. Find out what price discounts they offer for volume purchases. Then contact businesses directly. Have a flyer showing product you offer and prices, and tell them what the minimum order is. You can deliver to homes as well as by distributing flyers to homes, advertising on bulletin boards, PTA/PTO, local papers, schools. etc. (Make sure that your minimum order makes it worthwhile for you to deliver, and isn't too big

(ie.10 cases, otherwise you may not get many customers.)

MARGARITA MAGIC

Description Of Opportunity: You can liven up any party or social gathering with a Margarita machine. By charging a minimum amount for the rental and selling them the mix, you can make a tidy profit.

How Much Money To Start? $200 to $4,000

Equipment Needed: At least one Margarita machine, but preferably several. Margarita mix, and a van or pickup truck for delivery.

Can Opportunity Be Operated From Home? Yes

How Quickly Can It Be Up & Running? Within a month

Special Skills Or Knowledge: None. The Margarita mix is already pre-measured and ready to go.

Starting Your Business: You will need to locate a restaurant supply house or check in Thomas Registry for Margarita machine manufacturers. Buy one, two or three machines and plenty of Margarita mix! Advertise in local papers, supermarkets, PTA/PTO newsletters, company personnel office and bulletin boards (for company picnics and company gatherings of all sorts), organizational fund raisers (VFW, etc.), flyers to homes, gift shops, bakeries, etc. All you will have to do is deliver the machine and Margarita mix, teach the host how to operate the machine (if you aren't doing it yourself), come back after the party to get your equipment and pick up your check.

SELL SECONDS

Description Of Opportunity: You will need to locate businesses in your area that manufacture candy, cookies, brownies, muffins, etc. Most of these companies will sell items that do not come out perfect, ie. wrong shape, too big/small, broken, as seconds for a greatly reduced price.

How Much Money To Start? $200 and up

Equipment Needed: You will need a set of scales, packaging material, a price list, a product list.

Can Opportunity Be Operated From Home? Yes

How Quickly Can It Be Up & Running? Immediately

Special Skills Or Knowledge: None

Starting Your Business: You will need to contract to buy a certain amount (or eventually all) of the seconds that a company produces, for a greatly reduced price. Re-package these items in varying sizes, eg. 1/2 lb., 1 lb., etc. Then sell them below the price of the first line products. You can use the product name but clearly state that these items are seconds.

You have several avenues for marketing these packages: flea markets. Auctions (make certain to state that there is a "reserve"...a price below which they won't be sold...
This will guarantee you a profit...) Allow yourself a decent profit, taking into account that the auction house will charge you 10-25% for selling at their auction. At a good auction house you will sell most, if

not all, of your seconds.   Other ways to sell them directly are: hospital gift shops, thrift stores, distribute flyers in less affluent neighborhoods (telling them that you will deliver or be in a certain location at a given time each week), newspapers, bulletin boards in schools/places of worship, PTA/PTO meetings, etc.

THE SPICE OF LIFE

Description Of Opportunity: You will be buying large quantities of spices, eg. fajita spices, chili powders, specialty spices, and re-package them under your own company name. You will sell them individually or in bulk to other businesses.

How Much Money To Start? $200 to $1,000

Equipment Needed: You will need a set of scales, bottles or plastic containers or vacuum sealed bags, and your own labels.

Can Opportunity Be Operated From Home? Yes

How Quickly Can It Be Up & Running? Within 1 month

Special Skills Or Knowledge: A knowledge of spices is helpful but not essential. A knowledge of which spices work well with other spices will definitely help increase sales.

Starting Your Business: After re-packaging them, you can either sell them directly to individuals by mail order, advertise your business through local newspapers and on various bulletin boards, and through fund raising groups. The mail order business should grow nicely, especially if you offer specials, eg. a free package of spices to any current customer who refers a new buyer to you.
Another avenue is to market them in bulk, but under your label, to gourmet stores, gift shops, specialty stores, grocery stores, caterers, restaurants (if you can

show that your product is superior or fresher, than the spices that they are currently buying).

JELLY MAKER

Description Of Opportunity: You will be making fresh, homemade jams, jelly, marmalades, etc., emphasizing that your product is fresh and homemade.

How Much Money To Start? $200 and up

Equipment Needed: You will need a good mixer, jelly jars, lids, good recipes, professionally designed labels.

Can Opportunity Be Operated From Home? Yes

How Quickly Can It Be Up & Running? Immediately

Special Skills Or Knowledge: Some good recipes and a knowledge of canning methods. (Most cookbooks and some pectin boxes contain information on canning jelly.)

Starting Your Business: You must locate a good source of fruit for your business, have good recipes and then make up samples of various varieties. Decide if you want to market directly to the public or prefer selling via mail order or wholesale. If you want to retail directly to the public, flea markets, crafts shows, fairs are all good options. If you plan to wholesale, avenues are gourmet food stores, grocery stores, bakeries, gourmet restaurants, specialty stores, hospital gift shops, caterers, Mom and Pop stores and natural food stores. If mail order is your choice, you can combine this with retail by giving your customers catalogs for future orders. You can also sell your products on your computer to cooking clubs listed with various on-line providers. You can purchase mail order lists from various sources (check with your library). Ask everyone for a letter of recommendation, including friends and family, getting their written permission to use their opinion in future ads and publications.

You can expand your business by including meat relishes, other relishes, chutneys, etc.

BE A SPECIALTY DIET CHEF

Description Of Opportunity: You have several different areas that you can specialize in. You can locate people who need or want to be on a healthy diet. You can offer a menu or just daily specials, delivering the meal to your customers. Have them order at least 24 hours in advance. A more specialized approach, and possibly more profitable since there is less competition, is to offer your service to people convalescing after sickness or who have been released from the hospital, or people with special diets due to allergies, or people trying to lose or gain weight.

How Much Money To Start? $200-$300

Equipment Needed: Most of the equipment you will need comes from your own kitchen. Anything else you will need, including individual serving containers, can be purchased from a restaurant supply house. You will need a reliable vehicle and an answering machine, answering service or voice mail.

Can Opportunity Be Operated From Home? Yes

How Quickly Can It Be Up & Running? Within 1 week

Special Skills Or Knowledge: A good knowledge of various types of recipes, namely low sodium, low sugar, low fat, or low cholesterol. However, if you don't have that knowledge, there are many books in the library and in the bookstores, and from various organizations such as the Heart Association, that can provide you with approved menus.

Starting Your Business: If you wish to cater to people on health food diets, you will need to advertise in health food and natural food newspapers and shops in your local area. A more direct approach would be to advertise on billboards, chiropractors offices, with nutritionists, holistic medicine clinics, gyms, doctors offices who specialize in weight loss, etc. If you want to specialize in diets for people recovering from illness, surgery, or allergies; contact nurses, doctors, hospitals, chiropractors, etc., telling them of your service. You can also contact senior centers and doctors specializing in geriatric medicine. Advertise at places of worship (clergy frequently know of people in their own congregation who need special diets), PTA/PTO meetings/newsletters (PTO members have parents, who might need your service.

ICE CREAM SAUCE MAKER

Description Of Opportunity: We all know that ice cream is one of the most popular desserts in the country. You can successfully become part of this multimillion dollar business by making a wide variety of homemade, healthy, low fat, low sodium ice cream sauces. You can make one sauce, several varieties, develop unusual sauces or just produce high quality sauces that you believe will more than compete with the nationally advertised brands.

How Much Money To Start? $200 plus

Equipment Needed: Mixing bowls, jars, labels.

Can Opportunity Be Operated From Home? Yes

How Quickly Can It Be Up & Running? Within 30 days

Special Skills Or Knowledge: You must have, or develop, some wonderful ice cream sauce recipes. You may decide to start with recipes that are already popular or make your own unique sauces.

Starting Your Business: Your best approach would be to create several recipes eg. chocolate, fudge, strawberry, caramel, or make unusual combinations of sauces. When you have made and attractively packaged with your sauces, wholesale them to ice cream stores, gourmet stores, bakeries, food distributors, grocery stores, Mom & Pop stores, businesses that who sell ice cream at shows, fairs, conventions, flea markets, street festivals, etc. When you are established in the market, you can then approach ice cream makers directly and see if they are interested in adding your ice cream sauce to their distribution chain. Obviously you will have to sell to them at a discounted price, but in the long run, this could be very profitable for you.

POPCORN POPPER

Description Of Opportunity: Americans eat huge amounts of popcorn each year. You can easily pop right into this business by popping your own corn and flavoring it with caramel, cheese, butter, toffee, etc. You can also make unusual flavorings eg. barbecue, Cajun, etc. along with the basic flavors.

How Much Money To Start? $500 to get started

Equipment Needed: You will need to purchase a professional popcorn popper. You may be able to save money by locating a good used one, calling restaurant supply houses, asking them if they have any good used ones for sale. You will need large and small gift tins, and/or plastic bags and ties. You will need to buy popcorn, salt, flavored butter, oil or margarine in bulk.

Can Opportunity Be Operated From Home? Yes

How Quickly Can It Be Up & Running?   Within 1 week

Special Skills Or Knowledge: In order to get into this business you will have to experiment with your own recipes to determine the proper amount of flavorings to add to the popcorn. You can find additional flavoring ideas from cookbooks, friends and family.

Starting Your Business: Determine the different size packages and tins that you wish to use. Use packaging that is eye catching and attractive. Then you can wholesale your finished product to various outlets including grocery stores, gourmet outlets, schools, PTA/PTO, fund raisers, stores that specialize in movie rentals, hospital gift stores, etc. You can also retail them directly by setting up regularly at sporting events (baseball, soccer, etc.), fairs, car shows, flea markets, horse shows, and any events where there are lots of people. You can start a gourmet flavor of the month club...this will take a lot of time and effort, but will give you a regular clientele and a regular income.

You might want to include tins that have dividers inside, allowing you to sell multiple flavors at once. These are very popular at offices (ie. real estate offices. doctors' offices, etc...we know of one office that went from ordering one 10 gallon container of flavored popcorn a week to 2 10 gallon containers. The three most popular choices in this particular office were buttered, cheese and barbecue). Ask your customers which flavors they like best and if there are any flavors that they would like to try.

GOURMET ICE CREAM MAKER

Description Of Opportunity: You will be starting your own little ice cream business like (Ben and Jerry's). You can either start small and stay small or you can start small with the idea of expanding. The more unique or varied your product line, the greater chance you will have of achieving success.

How Much Money To Start? $1000 plus

Equipment Needed: You will need to purohase an ice cream maker. These can be found at restaurant supply houses. You will need to purchase containers, packaging material, coolers for delivery, a large freezer, cones and wafers, if you will be making individual servings.

Can Opportunity Be Operated From Home? Yes

How Quickly Can It Be Up & Running? Within 30 days

Special Skills Or Knowledge: You will need to know how to make ice cream. There are many books in the library on this subject. Come up with creative ideas for different flavors of ice cream or no fat/low calorie ice creams.

Starting Your Business: You have several choices. You can specialize in producing ice creams for movie houses that would like to sell unique "homemade" ice cream at their concession stand. This will give you a steady and regular group of customers. You can also sell to sporting arenas, including professional arenas, if you are determined and have an excellent product.

Convenience stores, gourmet stores, bakeries, people who sell at smaller sporting events, fairs, flea markets, craft shows, street festivals, school events, company picnics. Also companies that have ice cream trucks are potentially good customers.

If you plan to retail your product yourself, make sure that your location has lots of people walk by customers. Why? Because you will have to make lots of sales to make any real money. Tip: give your ice cream creations catchy names.

OPENING A THEME RESTAURANT

Description Of Opportunity: There are many ethnic or unique restaurants that you can open. Here are some ideas: Polish, African, Soul Food restaurants and ethnic restaurants that would appeal to your community and You!. Some ideas for unique restaurants would include: a mystery theater restaurant where you give your customers (included in the price of the meal,) a chance to participate in a murder mystery that is performed before, during and after the meal. Another idea: have a musical theme restaurant such as: opera, 40's, 50's, 60's, karaoke, country and western, any style of music that appeals to people in your local community. Another amusing idea is to have singing waiters and waitresses.

Costume parties are always great hits so why not open a restaurant that has a menu that reflects a specific period in history, a world event, a sports theme, etc. on a rotating basis. The guest with the best costume for the evening could get dinner free. This means that you must prepare the menu/theme well in advance for people to plan their attire. You may choose to have a restaurant that reflects a specific location, such as Hawaii. Your patrons dress in island attire, again with a prize. You might also include a fashion show, with the guests as the models (in their own clothes or with the assistance of a clothing store who exchanges clothes for advertising). If it is limited to the customers own clothing, you can call them up to model from their table during the meal, with the reward, a free dinner for the best dressed.
"Cook Your Own Food" restaurants are also very popular. This is where your customers usually cook

their food at their table, ie. Mongolian restaurants, Fondue restaurants.

How Much Money To Start? $5,000 and UP!

Equipment Needed: If your operate this out of your home, you may have the majority of the items necessary in your kitchen. However, you may need to add larger size pots and pans. If you are opening a restaurant that will not be in your home, you may need to purchase cooking utensils plus tables, chairs, plates, cutlery, glasses, linens, etc. You will have to pay to lease a building and any appliances. Your best option is to find a building that was previously a restaurant, and still has most of the equipment on site and working. Negotiate the equipment into the lease price of the building.

Can Opportunity Be Operated From Home? Yes and No.

How Quickly Can It Be Up & Running? At least 30 days

Special Skills Or Knowledge: Check with your local health department concerning licenses and regulations under which you will operate. Decide on a specific novelty or exclusive idea to make your restaurant stand out.

Starting Your Business: You can keep your overhead much lower if you can open the restaurant in your own home. You would live on the top floors, and operate your restaurant on the ground floor. There is a VERY successful restaurant called The Durham House, just south of Dallas in Waxahachi. They only serve dinner Wednesday through Saturday nights. You must book at least a month in advance due to the large and regular clientele. (And this isn't an inexpensive restaurant either.) The restaurant is in a residential neighborhood. The owners call you to confirm your reservation and to give you directions. Their waiting list is very long!!

You must check with zoning and health department regulations prior to beginning this venture. Having the business in your home limits your financial investment and risk. If you cannot, or do not wish to open a restaurant in your home, then, to save money, look for a location that is out of the way but will still attract a large number of people. A previous restaurant location with equipment still in place can save you money. However, check with the people in surrounding businesses to try and determine why the previous business didn't succeed. Maybe it was a bad location, no parking or limited access. If a restaurant isn't easy to get into, unless it is really spectacular, your customers may simply drive by.

Try looking at unique buildings, eg. an old fire house, a church, a warehouse, unusual shaped buildings, service stations with big bays and consider converting them. Also when you are driving around your neighborhood, look for buildings that have been vacant for a while, contact the realtor or leasing agent and see what kind of deal you can make. Try asking for 3 to 6 months free rent as an incentive for you to move in. This can give you a chance to get up and running without the additional overhead until you have established a regular clientele. If you do lease a service station, make sure it didn't close due to environmental problems. There may be regulations regarding opening a restaurant on a former service station lot, too.

Advertise an ethnic restaurant in ethnic newspapers, ethnic houses of worship, clubs, food stores, and flyers in ethnic neighborhoods. The same approach will work for music based restaurants, but advertised in music papers and businesses. Try a spotlight outside your restaurant that shines into the night and then advertise. "Look for Our Spotlight". For a mystery restaurant, you can also advertise at local theater groups and in the entertainment section of the newspaper.

Coupons work well. 2 for 1 coupons work well. Use 50% off coupons. This will encourage single people who may not want to invite someone to join them to use a 2 for 1 coupon. Today, many singles go out to dinner by themselves, so don't on this market.

MOBILE FOOD WAGON

Description Of Opportunity: If you live anywhere near construction sites, you've probably seen food wagons. They carry a variety of foods and beverages, everything from salads, sandwiches, burritos and yogurt to hot chocolate, tea, coffee and sodas. Some food wagons purchase their products from a food distributor. Others make their own entrees for a higher profit margin.

How Much Money To Start? From as little as $3,000 for a used wagon to a whole lot more for a new one.

Equipment Needed: A mobile food wagon. To keep your start up costs lower find a good used food wagon.

Can Opportunity Be Operated From Home? Yes

How Quickly Can It Be Up & Running? Within 30 days

Special Skills Or Knowledge: It would be helpful if you make most of your own foods, including salads, sandwiches, ethnic foods, desserts. It would definitely help if you, or someone in your family, had mechanical skills in case your food wagon needs repairs.

Starting Your Business: If you've ever driven past a construction site or new neighborhood, you've probably seen food wagon arriving at various times of the day, specifically early morning (around 7 AM), mid morning, (about 10 AM), lunch (noon or so), and mid afternoon (about 2 PM). These are the times that the construction workers take their breaks. This is when they will buy the food and drinks that you would provide. You can also serve office buildings where the employees may be on a tight budget or simply not have the time or inclination to go to a restaurant. They may bring part of their lunch and buy additional items from your food wagon. If you become known for a special type of food, perhaps ethnic, health food, great salads, unusual sandwiches, or low cost but great entrees, you might very well find yourself besieged by office employees.

BREAD ART

Description of Opportunity: Have you seen cookies made in various shapes? Well, you can create the same shapes, and others, such as rabbits, states, stars, cars, houses, children, interesting planes...almost anything you can imagine. By using different types of breads you can create different effects for many occasions.

How Much Money To Start? Under $200

Equipment Needed? Bread molds, your oven and your imagination

Can Opportunity Be Operated From Home? Yes

How Quickly Can It Be Up & Running? Literally, in just a day or two.

Special Skills Or Knowledge: You will need several good bread recipes, eg. rye, pumpernickel, etc. If you don't have any, you can experiment with recipes you find in cookbooks. You can either have the creative ability to make your own molds or you can find them at craft shops or cooking stores.

Starting Your Business: You'll need to make or buy a variety of unique molds. By taking pictures of the samples that you've made you create a photographic catalog of your ideas.   Then show them to caterers of weddings, bar mitzvahs, conventions, graduations, cocktail parties, etc.   You can also sell them to bakeries, supermarkets, delis, sandwich stores, etc.

BASKET LUNCHES

Description of Opportunity: Business people are always looking for a quick, convenient and tasty lunch. We know of people in Los Angeles who recognize this and are taking good advantage of this opportunity. They go down to the business communities and sell homemade sandwiches, salads, cookies, etc. which they carry in an attractive picnic basket. They are charging $2.50 to $5.00 for their sandwiches and salads. They are increasing their profit margin by selling their cookies and brownies for $1 to $2.00 a piece. Adding sodas, fruit juice and fruit will enable you to earn even more.

How Much Money To Start? Under $100

Equipment Needed: Picnic basket, coolers, vehicle. Everything else you need, you most likely have in your home.

Can Opportunity Be Operated From Home? Yes

How Quickly Can It Be Up & Running? Same day

Special Skills Or Knowledge: Creativity in making sandwiches and salads. Plus the ability to talk to people in a friendly way, or the ability to hire someone to do it for you.

Starting Your Business: Make up a variety of tasty and creative sandwiches, salads, cookies, brownies and anything else that would be ideal for lunch and be easy to carry. Purchase an attractive picnic basket and a large cooler. If you can't carry the picnic basket, a luggage carrier will help.

Simply go down to the business district about 11:00, dressed in an attractive outfit, and go office to office, selling your lunch items. We recommend that rather than just barging into an office, be sure to ask permission. If you smile and are friendly, they should not object. It would be a good idea to have a menu so they can see your selection and prices. Plus, by leaving one or more menus in each office you visit, you will find that this is a good way to have your customers call you in the future and order their lunches ahead of time, which will enable you to expand your business and increase your profits.

Note: you can simply type your menu on a typewriter or computer (if you don't have one, have a friend do it) and have them photocopied on white or colored paper.

MAKE YOUR OWN HORSERADISH

Description Of Opportunity: If you're like me and love the taste of strong horseradish, you know you can't find a good one at the supermarket among all those mass produced, watered down varieties. Here's your opportunity to fill this gap in the market by producing a fresh, great tasting, strong horseradish.

How Much Money To Start? Under $100

Equipment Needed? Bottles, labels, mixing bowl, and of course, HORSERADISH!

Can Opportunity Be Operated From Home? Yes

How Quickly Can It Be Up & Running? Less than 1 week

Special Skills Or Knowledge? If you don't have your own recipe for a horseradish that will BLAST your sinuses clean, then look through several recipe books and test several recipes to find the one you like best. If you don't like horseradish, try them on a friend who does.

Starting Your Business: After mixing, bottling and labeling your Horseradish Sauce, go around and market it to the following businesses: restaurants, delis, caterers, sandwich shops, specialty food stores, meat markets, supermarkets. Giving them samples to try themselves, will either convince them to stock your product, or knock their socks off.

Some cleaver ways to expand your business: do demonstrations in businesses where you allow customers to sample your horseradish, set up in food trade shows, or set up in flea markets, always looking to sell wholesale as well as retail.

PARTY COOK

Description Of Opportunity: You will be offering to prepare and cook for parties in various situations: in peoples homes, in offices, picnic locations, small wedding receptions, in fact anywhere that people get together and wish to have food served. You will be providing everything from cups and saucers, to cooking and serving the meal, and cleaning up afterwards.

How Much Money To Start? $200 to $2,000

Equipment Needed: Pots, pans, cutlery, dinnerware, glasses, portable propane cookers, coolers, white cloth tablecloths/napkins, white shirts, black skirts/trousers and a reliable vehicle.

Can Opportunity Be Operated From Home? Yes

How Quickly Can It Be Up & Running? Within 1 month

Special Skills Or Knowledge: You must be a good cook or you will have to hire a good cook who can work in limited space and under unusual conditions. You'll need a good personality, professional manner and appearance, and you must be friendly, and smile, SMILE, **SMILE!**

Starting Your Business: The most important thing about this business is letting people know that you are offering this service. You can look for advertising ideas in our chapter on advertising but some suggestions are: placing flyers on doors in affluent neighborhoods, putting notices on grocery store bulletin boards in those same neighborhoods, advertising in local papers that serve affluent areas, using bulletin boards in places of worship, and by word of mouth. Always call the hostess the next day to determine if they were happy with your service, ask if they would like to hire you again for their next party, and ALWAYS ask for referrals.

You will also be marketing your business directly to businesses. This can describe the service you are offering, either in person, over the phone, or with a colorful flyer through the mail. Be sure to contact businesses on many occasions so that they are familiar with your service especially around the holiday seasons.
Remember, persistence pays!

Another idea: contact large caterers. Tell them about your business, the types of food you prepare and ask them to contact you with catering jobs that are too small for them, or that they are not equipped to handle.

MEALS FOR SINGLES

Description Of Opportunity: There are many young singles, elderly singles, young couples, old couples, not to forget families, that would like to have homecooked meals, but either don't have the time or the ability to make them. This is where you come in. You offer them a menu, different for each day. You will deliver these hot meals to their home or apartment at a pre-arranged time.

How Much Money To Start? Under $300

Equipment Needed: You'll have most of the things that you'll need in your own kitchen, however you will need the following: individual foil lined containers to keep food hot, large hot/cold coolers (these you can find at restaurant suppliers). You will also need a reliable vehicle.

Can Opportunity Be Operated From Home? Yes

How Quickly Can It Be Up & Running? Within 1 week

Special Skills Or Knowledge? You must be a good cook with several good recipes and have the ability to cook in volume.

Starting Your Business: You will have to make up flyer menus and business cards and deliver these to apartment buildings, retirement communities, and residential neighborhoods. You can also post flyers in supermarkets, places of worship, gyms, etc. For regular customers, you can also make up refrigerator magnets from your business cards. These magnet backs are available through office supply stores/catalogs. They cost about $20 for 100 magnetic backs. If you want to have them in larger numbers at a larger cost, you can have them made professionally.

By having your weeks menu (with pricing) on your answering machine or voicemail box, new customers, can order ahead of time. For current customers, you can either mail them menus (with prices) for the coming week or month, or have them call your voicemail or answering machine. Another option is to leave the menu on their answering machine, or easier still, include a written menu for the week or month when you deliver their meal.

Price your meals to include food costs, preparation time, delivery costs, and your PROFIT. Do not make your initial delivery area too big. Later, if you wish to expand you can hire delivery drivers.

MARKET YOUR OWN RECIPE!

Description Of Opportunity: This is the simplest way for you to market old family recipes, or recipes all your friends are wild about! Simply place small classified ads in local papers, regional papers, magazines, etc. describing what the recipe is   eg.   salad dressing, chocolate cake, candy, barbecue sauce, etc. Include your name, address and price and watch the dollars roll in!

How Much Money To Start? Under $100

Equipment Needed: None

Can Opportunity Be Operated From Home? Yes

How Quickly Can It Be Up & Running? Same day

Special Skills Or Knowledge: A good recipe (or recipes) and the ability to write good classified ads.

Starting Your Business: Select newspapers, bulletin boards, magazines, etc. where you are likely to find mainly female readers. If one recipe is selling well, continue to advertise it. If your recipe isn't selling well, try rewording your ad. If that doesn't help, try another recipe. When people purchase one recipe, send them a list of other recipes that they can purchase from you. These additional sales will increase your profit margin without any additional advertising costs.

Ask people to let you know how they like your recipe. If one recipe seems to be a big hit, you might consider making it up and marketing the finished product yourself. (If you do decide to make and sell the final product, please check with your local Health Department to see if you need any licenses and to see what rules and regulations you may have to comply with.)

DOUGH FROM DOUGH!

Description Of Opportunity: In this day and age of mass produced foods, many people have never tasted or smelled freshly baked bread. If you love to bake, this is a perfect opportunity for you to rake in the dough!

How Much Money To Start? Initially, under $100.

Equipment Needed: Bread pans, wrappers, good recipes, trays, and a reliable vehicle. You may also consider purchasing a bread machine.

Can Opportunity Be Operated From Home? Yes

How Quickly Can It Be Up & Running? Immediately

Special Skills Or Knowledge: A selection of good bread recipes. eg. health food breaks, regional of ethnic breads, etc.

Starting Your Business: You can start this business small by simply selling to your family, friends and neighbors.

To expand, all you need to do is take samples to delis, caterers, sandwich shops, supermarkets, Mom & Pop stores, hospitals, and any other place that sells or uses lots of bread.

DEHYDRATED FOODS

Description Of Opportunity: You can easily track down surplus fruits, vegetables, herbs and flowers to dehydrate by contacting farmers, supermarkets, food wholesalers, and farmers markets. OR you can grow your own. Then vacuum pack the finished product, placing your label on the packaging.

How Much Money To Start? $100 to $500

Equipment Needed: You'll need a good, commercial dehydrator, plus packaging material. You can find all of these at a good restaurant supply house.

Can Opportunity Be Operated From Home? Yes

How Quickly Can It Be Up & Running? Within 1 month

Special Skills Or Knowledge: All you'll have to do is follow the manufacturers directions on your dehydrator and have attractive labels produced for your finished product.

Starting Your Business: You can market your dehydrated products to wholesale customers by taking, or mailing them, samples of your finished product line. Good markets will be supermarkets, sporting goods stores, camping supply stores, convenience stores, Mom and Pop stores, fishing stores, gun stores, health food stores, and survivalist stores.
If you wish, you can market your dehydrated products directly by advertising in specialty magazines you can very easily find yourself in the world of mail order. The best types of magazines would be the ones ready by

campers, hikers, hunters, survivalists, sportsmen, health food nuts.

Don't forget that your family, friends, and neighbors are also potential customers. Some religious groups such as Mormons could also be very good customers. Why? Because they believe strongly in storing a one year supply of food for their families and dehydrated foods store very well!

APPENDIX I

Purchase Order

P. O. Number:

Fax:

To:	Ship to (if different address):

P.O. DATE	PLACED BY	DATE EXPECTED	SHIP VIA	F.O.B.	TERMS

QTY.	DESCRIPTION	UNIT PRICE	TOTAL

SHIPPING & HANDLING	
SUBTOTAL	
SALES TAX RATE	
SALES TAX	
TOTAL DUE	

_____
Authorized Signature

Invoice

Invoice Number:
Date:

Fax:

To:	Ship to (if different address):

SALESPERSON	ORDER NO.	DATE SHIPPED	SHIPPED VIA	F.O.B.	TERMS

QTY.	DESCRIPTION	UNIT PRICE	TOTAL
			0.00
			0.00
			0.00
			0.00
			0.00
			0.00
			0.00

SUBTOTAL	0.00
SALES TAX RATE %	
SALES TAX	0.00
SHIPPING & HANDLING	
TOTAL DUE	$0.00

THANK YOU FOR YOUR ORDER!

Weekly Planner

Fax:

Monday	
8:00	
9:00	
10:00	
11:00	
12:00	
1:00	
2:00	
3:00	
4:00	
5:00	

Tuesday	
8:00	
9:00	
10:00	
11:00	
12:00	
1:00	
2:00	
3:00	
4:00	
5:00	

Things To Do This Week

Wednesday	
8:00	
9:00	
10:00	
11:00	
12:00	
1:00	
2:00	
3:00	
4:00	
5:00	

Thursday	
8:00	
9:00	
10:00	
11:00	
12:00	
1:00	
2:00	
3:00	
4:00	
5:00	

Notes

Friday	
8:00	
9:00	
10:00	
11:00	
12:00	
1:00	
2:00	
3:00	
4:00	
5:00	

Saturday

Sunday

Quarterly Cash Flow	1ST	2ND	3RD	4TH
OPERATING ACTIVITIES	$	$	$	$
NET CASH PROVIDED/USED BY OPERATING ACTIVITIES				
INVESTING ACTIVITIES	$	$	$	$
NET CASH PROVIDED/USED BY INVESTING ACTIVITIES				
FINANCING ACTIVITIES	$	$	$	$
NET CASH PROVIDED/USED BY FINANCING ACTIVITIES				
NET INCREASE/DECREASE IN CASH				
CASH AND EQUIVALENTS AT BEGINNING OF QUARTER				
CASH AND EQUIVALENTS AT END OF QUARTER				

Mileage Record

Fax:

Date:

Date	Start	Stop	Total Miles	Gas/Oil ($)	Parking/Tolls ($)	Misc. ($)
		Grand Totals				

Approved by:

Application For Employment

Fax:

Personal Information

Name:		Date:
Social Security Number:		
Home Address:		
City, State Zip:		
Home Phone:	Business Phone:	
US Citizen?	If Not Give Visa No. & expiration:	

Position Applying For

Title:	Salary Desired:
Referred By:	Date Available:

Education

High School (Name, City, State):	
Graduation Date:	
Business or Technical School :	
Dates Attended:	Degree, Major:
Undergraduate College :	
Dates Attended:	Degree, Major:
Graduate School:	
Dates Attended:	Degree, Major:

References